"This book is something extraordinary. Bob Ekblad combines theological competence with a dynamic Spirit-infused Christianity, grounded in a social passion for the poor and the marginalized. That is an expression of the kingdom of God, a demonstration of how Jesus is."

—STEFAN SWÄRD
Evangelical Alliance, Stockholm

"*The Beautiful Gate* is a book that you want to keep on reading and yet at the same time you want to stop mid chapter so you can flesh out what the book is saying. Its pages are full of the beautiful tension between challenge and invitation . . . and Bob does a legendary job at both challenging us and inviting us to pursue the life of Jesus that is available. The stories are moving and the theology convicting. I read, I cried, I smiled, and I'm heading to *The Beautiful Gate*. Bravo."

—CARLOS A. RODRÍGUEZ
author of *Simply Sonship* and *Drop the Stones*

# THE BEAUTIFUL GATE

Feb 2e, 2017

To Ron,
Keep seeing & entering Jesus
kingdom!

yours.

Bob

# THE BEAUTIFUL GATE

## Enter Jesus' Global
## Liberation Movement

## BOB EKBLAD

THE PEOPLE'S SEMINARY PRESS

The Beautiful Gate
Enter Jesus' Global Liberation Movement

The People's Seminary Press
P.O. BOX 410
Burlington, WA 98233
www.peoplesseminary.org

ISBN: 978-1-5408-1566-8

Made in the USA.

For Gracie, Isaac, Luke, and Anna

# Contents

Acknowledgements                                    xi

Preface                                             xiii

1   **Enter Through the Beautiful Gate**            **1**

2   **Prototype Disciples:**                        **21**
    Peter & John, Me & You

3   **Empowering Presence**                         **41**

4   **Authority, Faith, and Empowerment**           **69**

5   **Embracing the Rejected One:**                 **85**
    A Theology of the Cross

6   **Transformation in Whose Name?**               **109**

7   **Repentance and Conversion**                   **128**

8   **Persecution and Breakthrough**                **148**

    Bibliography                                    177

# Acknowledgments

I am especially grateful to the inmates of Skagit County Jail and Washington State Reformatory for being my reading partners and fellow witnesses of Jesus' transforming friendship. Special thanks also to my colleagues Julio Montalvo and Salvio Hernandez, who regularly read and study Scripture with me at Tierra Nueva in Burlington, Washington, and to David Calix in Minas de Oro, Honduras.I am also grateful to my colleagues in Tierra Nueva's men's jail and prison ministry, who were present with me during some of Bible studies mentioned in this book: Chris Hoke, Mike Neelley, Matt Malyon, David Westerlund, Roger Capron, and Mike Zosel-- and to the rest of our staff and worshipping community. This book has come out of our common mission. Thanks also to the staff at Skagit County Jail and Washington State Reformatory for their support of our ministry with inmates.

Special thanks to the following people for their support of this project. Jennifer Hendrix helped me with valuable editorial advice at the beginning. Adria Vizzi Holub did the final editing and proofreading. Roger Wilkinson, John Linton, and Brad Jersak offered helpful observations and encouragement throughout the writing process. I am grateful to Mike Surber for his design of the cover and to Christian Amondson for his help with the interior/exterior layout and final stages of publication.

Without the companionship of my wife and best friend Gracie, none of this would be possible.

# Preface

The first miracle after Jesus' ascension and Pentecost happens in Acts 3, when Peter and John heal a man lame from birth who sits outside the temple gate. The two disciples go up to the temple at the ninth hour, the hour of prayer (Acts 3:1). They are newly filled with the Holy Spirit, empowered to embody and proclaim God's transforming love the way Jesus did. They are also rooted in a growing community of believers who are experiencing awesome wonders and signs, who share their possessions, eat and pray together, and praise God (Acts 2:43-47). They are active participants in a new movement, and this is a catalytic moment. As Peter and John move towards the place of prayer at the "hour of prayer," they find themselves in the optimal spiritual posture for engaging in a Jesus-like mission.

Simultaneously, a man lame from birth is being carried along in the same direction towards the temple. His path intersects with Peter and John's at the gate—which we learn is called "beautiful"—and this explosive encounter sets the course for the future church. Preferential option for the poor and marginalized, respectful presence, relational connectedness, empowerment, and physical healing in Jesus' name coalesce. The man is healed and joins Peter and John to cross the line of exclusion through the Beautiful Gate.

Once on the inside of the gate, Peter and John's audience and strategy change as they find themselves among the religiously qualified. New challenges come as advocates and the newly-included find themselves in the company of the excluders. Worship, inclusion, and gathering set the stage for preaching. This is the place and time for prophetic challenge. The activists expose the mechanisms and perpetrators of exclusion and death, and call people to repentance, conversion and into their highest destinies as positive change agents. The movement makes significant gains in adherents, challenging the status quo. This results in Peter and John's incarceration, persecution by the authorities, and the first community's eventual scattering for a broader mission to the nations.

There is no consensus among scholars about the location of the *Beautiful Gate*, and nowhere in Scripture is one of the temple gates so called. The Greek name *hōraios* means "belonging to the right hour or season" or "timely," and includes the notion of "flourishing," and by implication "beautiful." This definition evokes Isaiah 52:7 as the Apostle Paul quotes it in Romans 10:15: "How will they preach unless they are sent? Just as it is written, 'How beautiful [*hōraios*] are the feet of those who bring good news of good things.'" The term "gate" or "door" is often used to describe an entry point for proclamation of good news.[1] These texts suggest that the *beautiful gate* (or *beautiful door*) is symbolic of the timely or optimal threshold for encounters with God, where outsiders are met, transformed, and brought inside.

The Gospels tell of Jesus crossing the line in *beautiful gate*-like encounters with a wide array of people. These stories provide the inspiring templates for both Peter and John as they give their lives to following Jesus after Pentecost, and for you and me today as we are invited to do the same.

I regularly experience these timely encounters at the *beautiful gate* in jails, prisons, streets, and diverse locations here in Skagit County and around the world. I have had many encounters with individuals like the lame man, who live on the margins of religious institutions, and who are not looking for God.

This book is a call to follow Jesus through the *beautiful gates* of our times and out into the broken world. Herein lies an invitation to join a movement of holistic liberation that is empowered by the Holy Spirit. There is an urgency to this call, which is echoed by Jesus' words in Matthew 7:13-14, "Enter through the

1. 1 COR. 16:9; 2 COR. 2:12; COL. 4:3; REV. 3:20.

narrow gate; for the gate is wide and the way is broad that leads to destruction, and there are many who enter through it."

This book draws inspiration from Peter and John's first miracle without Jesus physically by their side. May you be inspired by these stories from life and Scripture, and experience a life of transforming encounters!

# 1

# Enter Through the Beautiful Gate

The *beautiful gate* is an impassable barrier separating the excluded from restoration, which suddenly becomes a doorway into a transformed life through divine engagement. These gates are more specifically encounters at the margins when God's intervention mediated through Jesus' followers moves someone rejected across a barrier into acceptance, healing, and empowerment. The prospect of transformation for someone barred opens a doorway of hope that includes anyone, anywhere, anytime.

Jesus' disciples, Peter and John, participate in a transformational encounter at the Beautiful Gate in Acts 3 that brings healing, joy, and full inclusion to a man lame from birth. Healing of the lame was foretold by Israel's prophets as a sign of the Messianic Kingdom, as in Isaiah 35:6: "Then shall the lame man leap as a deer, and the tongue of the stammerers shall speak plainly; for water has burst forth in the desert, and a channel of water in a thirsty land."[1] Jesus himself alerts John the Baptist to the fulfillment of this prophesy in his own ministry: "Go and report to John what you have seen and heard: the blind receive sight, the lame walk, the lepers are cleansed, and the deaf hear, the dead are raised up, the poor have the gospel preached to them" (Luke 7:22). In Jesus' Kingdom, the officially-excluded lame are deliberately included on the invitation list for the banquet in the

1. Lancelot C. L. Brenton, trans., *Septuagint* (London: Samuel Bagster & Sons, 1851).

Kingdom of God.[2] Peter and John are prototype Christians who embody the continuation of Jesus' Messianic Kingdom in his physical absence after his ascension and Pentecost, pointing the way forward for us.

In my ministry with Tierra Nueva, *beautiful gates* take many forms, including street corners, fields, courtrooms, and literal prison doors. In the Gospels, Jesus continually brings excluded people across thresholds marked "no entry," serving as border crosser, *coyote*, trafficker par excellent into his Kingdom. Before examining Acts 3 up close, let's look at some of Jesus' encounters in Luke's Gospel.

## JESUS CALLS NOTORIOUS CRIMINALS THEN AND NOW

In the Gospel of Luke we see Jesus modeling to Peter and John and all future disciples his barrier-transgressing approach in the calling of another disciple, Matthew, at a *beautiful gate* in Luke 5:27-32. Levi (Matthew) is a tax collector, despised by and alienated from his religious community. Jesus finds him sitting at his tax booth, his workplace, equivalent to the fishermen's boat or the lame man's begging spot at the temple gate.

"What was Levi doing when Jesus called him?" is a question that nearly always surprises people accustomed to seeing God's call as addressed to the righteous and deserving.

"He was sitting at his tax office collecting taxes" is an answer that opened a beautiful gate into an encounter among Spanish-speaking gang members in a Guatemalan prison.

I traveled to Guatemala to help a ministry train chaplains to incarcerated gang members, which included leading Bible studies with inmates in two maximum-security prisons. A few days before leaving, I had a vivid vision in the middle of the night of a heavily-tattooed Latino man with a hole in his right side.

The first prison we visited was surrounded by tanks and guards, to prevent rescue or escape. We were ushered through

2. Luke 14:13, 21.

barred entryways by guards in riot gear into the main section of a prison reserved for one particular Guatemalan street gang. We entered their cellblock alongside two prostitutes through a final set of prison doors. We found ourselves in the middle of a chaotic corridor bustling with inmates.

Our hosts managed to gather a small group of inmates at the far end of the hallway, where we would attempt to get away with a *beautiful gate* encounter through reading and discussing a story from the Bible and praying. Behind me was a curtained door that competed for people's attention, as men met with the prostitutes with whom we had entered. Young men sauntered across our circle while taking drags off their cigarettes or pretending to talk on cell phones, trying to take into their thirsty souls whatever they could while avoiding any appearance of being interested. Many were shirtless, sporting elaborate gangster tattoos on their chests, backs, and faces. I saw no one with a detectable hole in his right side, like the man in my vision.

The next day, two colleagues and I headed to one of Central America's most notorious prisons known for scandals and assassinations. There, behind razor-wire topped walls, members of another rival gang were imprisoned. The guards led us between walls with murals depicting Jesus at the table with his disciples at the Lord's Supper to ominous barred doors with an armed guard. Once through this gate, we were left unaccompanied with about 100 inmates.

We hung out and talked with a few men in the prison courtyard, including a man identified as the main leader. He went by the name of Psycho. He explained to me that many of the older inmates had lost their fathers to the death squads or the wars in Central America in the 1980s. Large numbers of young men and women adrift and afraid had migrated as young teens to the United States. Many had first joined these gangs there, where they started, in Los Angeles. Drug-dealing and other crime landed them in the California prison system, and subsequently in the hands of US immigration, who deported them back to their countries of origin. In Guatemala, El Salvador, and Honduras these gangs flourished, taking root in the fertile soil of fatherlessness, unemployment, social class divisions, and rampant violence. Most of the inmates were more recent recruits, and many more hadn't been so fortunate to make it to prison, having been killed by police. He went on to share how many are shot or incarcerated simply because of their tattoos, and that law enforcement blames them for everything wrong in their country, including their own crimes.

When the conversation lulled, I asked where I could find a bathroom. An inmate named Shark, with tattoos all over his chest, offered to guide me to the nearest toilet. Our host whispered that Shark was the other main leader, right as I noticed a gaping scar on his right side and realized this was the man of my vision two nights prior. I followed him with pounding heart into the dark recesses of the prison, searching for clues as to what the Spirit was expecting from me, as I inquired silently in prayer.

After stepping out of the bathroom, Shark humbly asked me if I'd like to see his cell. I agreed, and followed him through a narrow corridor. He stopped at the open door of his cell and warmly invited me to enter, motioning for me to take a seat on a plastic chair. Rap music was throbbing from his boom box, which he immediately turned down a bit so we could talk. I asked him about his scar, and he told me he'd been shot in his lower abdomen by the police in a confrontation and had nearly died. He had eventually recovered after months in the hospital. Subsequently he had been sentenced to 120 years and imprisoned.

I told him about the vision I'd had in the middle of the night two nights before at home in Washington State. How I'd seen a man with tattoos on his chest and a hole in his right side. I told him that I had been looking for someone matching his description. He was visibly moved. I explained that I didn't know why God might have wanted us to meet, but that since I am a pastor and regularly pray for people, that I would be glad to pray for him for anything that was on his heart.

"As a gang leader in prison, I imagine there must be lots of stress and a need for wisdom and clear direction," I continued. "Is there anything you need prayer for?" I asked.

I offered him a CD of worship music that I'd happened to bring, and a copy of my book, *Reading the Bible with the Damned*, which he warmly accepted. He immediately reached up to turn off the rap music, even as I insisted that it was fine to keep it on. But he insisted on playing the CD I'd brought him, and contemplative flute music filled the cell. I prayed for his son's health, and for his wife, and blessed him with God's love and peace.

God's presence was palpable, warming us like a campfire there in his cell. I asked him if he noticed anything, and he said he felt a lot of peace and he felt good. I told him that I believed we were experiencing Jesus, who came and still comes to show God's love and friendship to the poor and brokenhearted, and to sinners. I shared with him how I believe Jesus would gladly be there with him 24/7 if he welcomed him to take up residence there in his cell, in his life, inside his heart. I explained how he wants full agreement because he's not about being pushy, but is all about respect. He humbly nodded and said he wanted Jesus to be with him from then on. We prayed together, and he welcomed Jesus into his cell and into his life. All of this took place in a matter of minutes while people waited in the courtyard for a planned gathering.

From there I followed Shark back to the main prison courtyard, and we went straight into a gathering of forty or so inmates. The chaplains introduced us. After an opening prayer inviting the Spirit's presence, I told them that we believed Jesus was on their side and introduced a song my Tierra Nueva colleague Chris had written, "Jesus, Friend of Sinners." I asked the men if it was okay for my Tierra Nueva partner from Honduras, David, and I to go around and pray silently over each of them while Chris sang. The gang leaders nodded their approval, and the men all seemed agreeable, so we proceeded. God's presence came strongly as David and I went a step further and asked permission to lay hands on each person around the circle while Chris sang: "Jesus, friend of sinners, we love you."

Then I introduced my proposed Bible study on Jesus' call of Levi in Luke 5:27-39. I described how Levi (Matthew) was a tax collector—a member of a notorious class of people that nearly everyone hated. Jesus went right to where he worked, transgressing the established barrier between the bad guys and good guys of his time.

"Who might fit the description of tax-collectors today?" I asked. Gangs in Guatemala force business owners in their territories to pay "protection taxes" (for protection from themselves) and taxi drivers to pay "road taxes." The men smiled wryly and looked sideways at each other or down at the floor, subtly acknowledging that they fit the description.

"So what was Levi doing when Jesus called him?" I ask. The men look surprised when they noticed that he wasn't following any rules, seeking God, or doing anything religious, but practicing his despised trade when Jesus showed up on the street and chose him.

"So let's see if Jesus made Levi leave his gang to be a Christian," I suggest. At this point the men are expecting to hear the traditional Guatemalan Christian insistence that gang members must leave their gang as a prerequisite for following Jesus. I encourage people to look closely at the next verse, Luke 5:29. Jesus is eating at Levi's house with other tax collectors and sinners and the disciples.

"So who followed whom?" I ask, excited to see people's reaction. The men could see that Jesus had apparently followed gangster Levi into his *barrio* (neighborhood), where his *homies* (fellow gang members) joined him for a meal. We read the account of Mark 1:15 at this point, as it shows the extent of Jesus' hanging with the homies: "And many tax-gatherers and sinners were dining with Jesus and his disciples; for there were many of them, and they were following him."

"So what do you think, guys—would you let Jesus join your gang like Levi did?" I ask, looking directly to the two gang leaders.

"*Esta loco!*" ("That's crazy!") Shark exclaimed, laughing. The other main leader smiled and looked befuddled.

Next, we read about how the Pharisees and their scribes began grumbling at Jesus' disciples, asking, "Why do you eat and drink with the tax collectors and sinners?" I describe how Pharisees and scribes were the religious leaders, and asked them if religious and political leaders in Guatemala would be glad if Jesus came to Guatemala and joined them on their gang turf. The connections between first-century Palestine and contemporary Central America were becoming clear. I pointed out how Jesus directly challenged law-abiding people's pride and superiority, which obviously pleased the inmates.

I worried a bit about how my audience would react to Jesus' immediate response to the Pharisees' distain: "It is not those who are healthy who need a physician, but those who are sick." I asked them whether they were at all offended to think of themselves as sick, but there was no hint of outrage on anyone's face. In leading Bible studies on this story elsewhere, inmates have never been offended but often freely confess: "We are sick!" When I ask them what sicknesses they need Jesus to heal them from, they have often surprised me with their transparency, mentioning greed, anger, pain, addictions, legal troubles, relationship problems, hepatitis C, and the like.

There, in the Guatemalan prison, the inmates were much more guarded, but I knew that we'd made it through a critical moment. I had their attention, and Jesus' final word to the religious insiders in Matthew's account of this story hit these guys like a spray of spiritual bullets from a spiritual drive by: "Go and learn what this means, 'I desire mercy, not sacrifice.' For I have come to call not the righteous but sinners" (Matt. 9:13). In the special account in Matthew's Gospel, Jesus orders the religious leaders to leave Levi's house, expelling them. "Go and learn!" He excludes the rejecters and chooses the rejected ones, recruiting them into his ministry. Though the men's faces were expression-less, I knew from experience they were letting Jesus inside and hearing his call to follow. The *beautiful gate* had swung wide open, like the gates of hell.

## JESUS' EMBRACE OF THE REJECTED INVITES OURS

Jesus' pursuit of Matthew is fully aligned with his declaration about himself at the inauguration of his mission in his home-town synagogue in Nazareth during his public reading of Isaiah 61:1-2: "The Spirit of the Lord is upon me, and he has anointed me, to preach the Gospel to the poor, he has sent me to proclaim release to the captives, and recovery of sight to the blind, to set free those who are downtrodden, to proclaim the favorable year of the Lord."

Jesus declares this scripture fulfilled in the hearing of his hometown. Then he scandalizes his attentive neighbors by high-lighting the notoriously unworthy beneficiaries of two of Israel's most celebrated prophets.

The prophet Elijah is sent to an impoverished widow across Israel's border in pagan Zarephath at a time when there were many Israelite widows. At a time when there were many lep-ers in Israel, Elisha is led to heal Naaman, an enemy military commander from Syria afflicted with the disease. Certainly a gang leader, drug cartel kingpin, or jihadist leader could be seen as contemporary equivalents of Naaman. Jesus' preference for the excluded and for national enemies gets him cast out of his hometown, after which he begins his ministry in Capernaum.

Many ministry workers the world-over align themselves with Jesus' outward-focused mission to unreached people. Iven and Kashmira Hauptman make their home in the heart of one of Bangkok's most infamous red-light districts. I have accompanied Iven on the several-hour loop that he and Kashmira regularly walk between 10 p.m. and 1 a.m., ministering to men involved in male prostitution, who walk the streets around the Grand Palace and Temple of the Emerald Buddha.

Much like the lame man begging for alms outside the Beautiful Gate in Jerusalem, these young men were outside what is perhaps the most important national temple of Thailand. Like the lame beggar, they come not to worship, but to make money in a way that is viewed as shameful and inappropriate among religious people. Iven commented that when a Thai television crew made a video about their work a few years ago, the host was visibly upset by the sight of a used condom on the ground outside the wall of smaller temple in the neighborhood, and he commented on how much "disrespect" it would take to have sex next to such a "holy place."

Late at night downtown Bangkok was bustling, but around the Temple of the Emerald Buddha the streets were mostly desolate, with lone individuals or pairs of young men who stood on corners or at bus stops while cars slowly cruised past. When we first approached the young men (most between eighteen and thirty), they assumed we were customers. I followed Iven's lead in initiating contact, as he is fluent in Thai, and a veteran ministry worker in this neighborhood. He interpreted for me when I had something to say. On one outing we tried different ways of explaining our mission, and ended up repeating an explanation that seemed to take us the farthest in conversations and prayers.

First, we introduced ourselves, asked them their names, and where they were from. Some told us they were university students and need to do this kind of work to pay for their studies. They in turn asked us where we were from, and what we were doing there. We explained that we believe in a God who is especially looking for people who haven't been able to follow religious rules and consequently feel disqualified from salvation. We told them that we are there as emissaries sent by God to share good news about God's total love for them.

When given the opportunity, we sought to explain simply and clearly what we thought was the essential message, which went something like this: "God longs to show his love for you so much that he will himself go out to find you no matter where you are or what you are doing. God is looking for you not to punish you but to embrace, heal, forgive, and call you to a new life. We believe God did this most directly through his son, Jesus, who was born and lived on earth to demonstrate God's love and special care for people that the world considered failures—the poor and outcasts. Jesus offers total forgiveness for your sins, healing for your sicknesses, and he invites you to join him on his mission. Crowds followed Jesus when he was here. The religious leaders didn't like that he defended and helped the people that didn't obey the rules. They denounced him as a criminal and pressured the government to execute him. God raised him from the dead and we believe he is alive now and walks these streets with us. We are his followers and feel inspired to do exactly what he did."

We asked the young men whether they wanted or needed prayer for anything, and found that nearly everyone wanted to be prayed for. We prayed as cars with potential customers cruised slowly by, checking us out. The men were often distracted by this, as they felt pressured to make money. Iven told each person where he lives, and welcomed them to his storefront ministry center a few blocks away—another *beautiful gate* where Iven and his family live in the midst of a despairing neighborhood.

## JESUS' VETTING OF THE WORTHY

Skagit County Jail's multipurpose room is my most frequented *beautiful gate*. This room's three steel doors are manned from the Control Room, and allow correction officers, inmates, and ministry workers into a drab, tan-colored cinderblock space with a wall of bookshelves filled with tattered paperbacks where we gather in a circle to read and discuss the Bible and to pray—always under surveillance. On Thursday nights we hold four thirty-minute gatherings with inmates from different pods and tiers. On Sunday afternoons we have two gatherings.

The Gospels are filled with stories about Jesus' meetings with different individuals who would have been considered unworthy of God's special attention and love. Paying careful attention to the details of how Jesus encounters people in these stories can help flesh out what his ministry could look like today. Throughout Luke's Gospel we see Jesus ministering primarily in public, non-religious places to people mostly labeled as unworthy by religious leaders. He teaches beside the seashore, in cities, in homes, along the road. In Luke 6, he chooses his twelve disciples while in prayer on a mountain, and then descends to a level place where he welcomes crowds who come to be healed of their diseases and freed from unclean spirits (Luke 6:17). Reading the Gospels regularly with inmates sheds fresh light on these familiar stories—because inmates often find themselves in awkward, inhospitable, or even adversarial circumstances that parallel those of people Jesus helped.

We read the story of the Roman centurion in Capernaum, whose beloved slave is about to die. I briefly describe to the inmates how Roman soldiers were an occupying force that controlled and dominated ordinary Jewish people in Israel in Jesus' day, and that they were feared and hated because of their brutality. A centurion commanded one hundred soldiers. I ask the men to identify contemporary Roman centurions, and they mention prison wardens, sheriffs, prosecutors, drug task force chiefs, gang leaders, and drug cartel higher-ups.

We read about how he sends some Jewish elders to ask Jesus to come and save his slave's life. We notice together that the Jewish elders come to Jesus, insisting on the centurion's worthiness: "He is worthy for you to grant this to him; for he loves our nation, and it was he who built us our synagogue" (Luke 7:4-5). Jesus goes to his house. I ask the men if they think Jesus is going because he thinks the centurion is worthy.

I know from years of experience that people in crisis often try to make themselves as worthy as possible when they really need God's help. I find myself doing this too. There seems to be a deep-seated assumption in most people's thinking that God is like a probation officer or judge, looking to see if people are complying with requirements, evaluating evidence proving innocence or signs of measuring up to demands. Even if people claim to believe that God saves by grace, when we really need a miracle, we will make sacrifices perceived as pleasing to God. Inmates might make a special effort to clean up their language, confess all their sins, not miss a service, read the Bible more than usual, pray a lot, offer answers they perceive to be right in Bible studies, forgive enemies, fast—anything. The Jewish elders reflect this exhausting theology. They emphasize the centurion's merits to Jesus. We don't yet know whether Jesus goes with them because he thinks the centurion deserves it. All we know is that Jesus is on his way to this pagan Roman centurion occupier's house to heal (rather than free) one of his slaves.

We read on, looking for clues about what's really happening here. An older, grey-bearded inmate missing half his teeth is ecstatic. He has been reading ahead and wants us all to know the good news he's found. He doesn't think that the Roman centurion told the Jewish elders to tell Jesus about how worthy he was because he helped to build their synagogue. He argues that the Jewish elders advocated for the centurion based on their own belief that people have to be worthy to have their prayers answered. He thinks the Jewish elders want the centurion's ongoing help for their projects, and they do their best to convince Jesus to help them "pay him back" by healing his slave. Everyone is curious now to read the next verses to see what in fact is going on and whether there is good news for them, or confirmation of their negative suspicions.

The story clearly states that as Jesus draws closer to the centurion's house, the centurion sends his friends (people other than the Jewish elders) to tell Jesus that he is *not* worthy. Friends go now rather than the elders—not the beneficiaries of the centurion's charity. They speak as representatives of their friend: "Lord, do not trouble yourself further, for I am not worthy for you to come under my roof; for this reason I did not even consider myself worthy to come to you" (Luke 7:6-7a).

"Does the centurion's confession of his unworthiness keep Jesus from healing his slave?" I ask the men.

"Does Jesus say to the centurion's friends, 'Hey, wait a minute, I thought this guy was worthy, a righteous man deserving of a miracle. Since he's not, tell him to forget it!'?'"

The men laugh, in part, because it's dawning on them that this is not the case. Jesus has another very different attitude that we've yet to fully grasp. We need to read the next few verses to learn the final outcome of the story. The centurion's friends pass on his detailed request, which reveals his faith that Jesus' grace and love will trump his unworthiness: "But say the word, and my servant will be healed. For I, too, am a man under authority, with soldiers under me; and I say to this one, 'Go!' and he goes; and to another, 'Come!' and he comes; and to my slave, 'Do this!' and he does it" (Luke 7:7b-8).

I find myself amazed that the centurion doesn't present his best self to Jesus through his friends, in contrast to the Jewish elders' advocacy. He gives Jesus examples from his daily life as a Roman military commander who gives orders to soldiers who occupy Jesus' homeland. He doesn't give examples of his efforts in building Capernaum's synagogue, capitalizing on the Jewish elders' earlier appeal. Nor does he hide, or in any way minimize, having a slave. Rather, he even uses his ordering of his slave as an example of the authority he has over people in a pagan hierarchical domination system. You could almost say that the centurion uses real examples from his "life of crime" to show that he understands Jesus' authority as king in the Kingdom of God. Jesus marvels at this man, and publically states to the crowd and his disciples: "I say to you, not even in Israel have I found such great faith" (Luke 7:9).

In my past reading of this story, I have always thought of the centurion's exemplary faith as merely his belief that Jesus could heal from a distance with a word, giving an order to eradicate sickness, which, by itself, remains true and noteworthy. While Jesus certainly is able to do this, and does so in other Gospel stories, today I am seeing something new in our circle at the threshold of Skagit County Jail's *beautiful gate*. The older man with white hair reads the final verse: "And when those who had been sent returned to the house, they found the slave in good health" (Luke 7:10).

Together with the inmates, we find ourselves marveling at the extreme humility of both the centurion and Jesus. The centurion doesn't clean up his image to get Jesus' help, but presents himself the way he is, trusting in Jesus' mercy. Jesus does not publically speak a word of healing from a distance to impress the crowd, the Jewish elders, or the centurion's friends. Jesus doesn't model the authority that the centurion exemplifies. The centurion's friends find the slave well, without Jesus having taken any credit for the miracle. Instead, Jesus gives the "enemy" centurion credit for modeling something he calls faith, which we try to get our minds around in the final minutes of our jail Bible study before the guards come.

"How does this story speak to you guys today?" I ask the men. "What do you hear God saying to you as we've been reading and discussing?"

"The centurion knows he's unworthy, but asks Jesus for a miracle anyway," someone says. "We can do that now here in jail, and this gives me hope that Jesus will answer even when I don't have my life together and don't deserve help."

"Jesus is willing to go where the centurion lives, whether he is worthy or unworthy," someone else says.

We talk about faith as an assurance that we can appeal to Jesus for concrete and immediate help as we are in our undeserving state, without having to clean up our acts, and we can count on him coming to us wherever we are. We spend the last few minutes in prayer, thanking Jesus that he's already on his way towards us, whether others are praying for us, or we are asking for help ourselves. I invite the men to dare to make their requests known to Jesus, regardless of their current situation. On a weekly basis, men share stories of God answering their prayers in ways that bring them into an increasingly expectant faith.

## JESUS' RE-ENTRY AS THE NEW JOSHUA AT ISRAEL'S 'BEAUTIFUL GATE'

In another gathering with inmates, we look at Jesus' encounter in the city of Jericho with two other rejected ones: a blind beggar and a rich tax collector. I briefly describe how the ancient city of Jericho has long been associated with conquest. In the Old Testament, Joshua led the Israelite army into the city, where they slaughtered all the men, women, children, and animals (Josh. 2-6). I tell how on a 2013 visit to Jericho, I could see that the city is still associated with conquest, as the Palestinians live under Israeli occupation. I share how a big red warning sign posted by the Israeli military prohibited all Israeli citizens from entering the Palestinian city due to ongoing conflicts arising largely from aggressive Joshua-inspired Jewish settlements in the West Bank.

I invite the men to see how Jesus enters Jericho in Luke 18:35ff. I tell them how Jesus' name in Greek is spelled exactly the same as Joshua's name in the Greek Old Testament (Septuagint), ΔIhsouvß. So how does the entry of Jesus the Son of God into Jericho differ from that of Joshua son of Nun?

As Jesus approaches Jericho, "a certain blind man was sitting by the road, begging," someone reads from Luke 18:35. When he hears from the crowd that Jesus of Nazareth is passing by, he cries out: "Jesus, *son of David*, have mercy on me" (emphasis mine). The blind man "sees" Jesus as David's son, meaning the Messiah. In the face the of the crowd's attempt to silence and exclude him, Jesus orders the crowd to bring the blind man to him. Jesus shows preferential honor to the blind man, asking him: "What do you want me to do for you?" The blind man responds: "Lord, I want to regain my sight" (Luke 18:41). The blind man calls him *Lord*, using the Greek equivalent of the divine name. Jesus heals the blind man, who then follows him across the city line into Jericho. Everyone glorifies God.

This scene in Luke continues, and introduces another character from Jericho, Zaccheus, in Luke 19. In a jail Bible study one Sunday, I invite inmates to summarize what we know about

Zaccheus. He is a chief tax collector who is very rich, and too short to see Jesus over the crowd (Luke 19:2). I briefly describe a chief tax collector as a despised collaborator with oppressors, and invite comparisons. The inmates come up with a number of contemporary equivalents: undercover cops, drug cartel chiefs, agents from Immigration and Customs Enforcement (ICE), and debt collectors. We discuss Zaccheus' reaction to Jesus' entry into Jericho. The men point out his curiosity and possible desperation, since he runs ahead and positions himself deliberately in a tree to check Jesus out.

"Some of you may be coming to the Bible study to check out Jesus from a distance," I suggest, looking around the circle of men. Let's see what happens in the next verse: "And when Jesus came to the place, he looked up and said to him, 'Zaccheus, hurry and come down, for today I must stay at your house'" (Luke 19:5).

The men are surprised by Jesus' total awareness of Zaccheus' interest. I suggest the idea that Jesus could be a kind of bounty hunter, deliberately looking for people who have active warrants from heaven, perhaps due to their known interest or readiness. The inmates comment on how Jesus knew Zaccheus' name, told him to hurry and come down, and invited himself to stay at his house. Jesus "looks up" to Zaccheus in this encounter—and for a person "short of stature," who is also despised, this would have deeply affected him. The men are moved that Jesus doesn't judge him, and outdoes Zaccheus in his eagerness to know him. Jesus doesn't waste any time either, but sets the hook quickly into this wily fish, lest he get away. The scandal of Jesus' inclusion of Zaccheus is made clear by the reactions of the witnesses: "They *all* began to grumble, saying, 'he has gone to be the guest of a man who is a sinner'" (Luke 19:7, emphasis mine).

In this encounter, Jesus models his instructions to the seventy-two missionaries he sent out earlier, to look for the person of peace with whom they are to stay as guests (Luke 10:7). Zaccheus responds enthusiastically to Jesus' request to be his guest: "He hurried and came down, and received him gladly"

(Luke 19:6). Jesus' response invites further connection with Luke 10:8: "And whatever city you enter, and they receive you, eat what is set before you; and heal those in it who are sick, and say to them, 'The kingdom of God has come near to you.'" But before Jesus heals or announces the Kingdom, this notorious "criminal" identifies him as *Lord*, just as the blind man had on the outskirts of the city. Restorative justice is taking place spontaneously in Zaccheus in response to Jesus' full embrace: "Lord, half of my possessions I will give to the poor, and if I have defrauded anyone of anything, I will give back four times as much" (Luke 19:8). "Today salvation has come to this house," Jesus says, "because he too is a son of Abraham" (Luke 19:9).

Here Jesus reveals himself as the people of Jericho's Savior, illuminating the earlier First Testament Joshua conquest story and providing the key for appropriating it now. Unlike Joshua who destroyed Jericho, the new Joshua, Jesus, comes on a campaign to save: "For the Son of Man has come to seek and to save that which was lost" (Luke 19:10). He begins by bringing a blind beggar across the line into town, and continues in pursuit of the most wayward of its Jewish residents.

Luke's choice of words brilliantly connects Jesus to the spies sent by Joshua to view the land rather than to Joshua himself, whose actions destroy the city. Jesus, like the spies, has his eyes open to seek, but with a clear agenda to save. He *enters* and *stays* with Zaccheus—who is the equivalent of Rahab the prostitute, a direct ancestor of King David and Jesus (Matt. 1:5), with whom the spies take refuge. Zaccheus' timely reception of Jesus matches Rahab's reception of the spies (James 2:25); in both stories, those actions lead to salvation. I end the jail Bible study by returning to Jesus' urgency in connecting with Zaccheus and today's equivalents—us!

"From this text it looks to me like Jesus is looking to connect with people who are drawn to him. If you are experiencing a desire to receive this Jesus who is pursuing you, maybe it's time to seize the moment and hurry to welcome him as Zaccheus did," I suggest. Jesus continues his journey all the way to his arrest and crucifixion in Jerusalem, embodying salvation to those outside the gate.

Readers should also note that right before this story, Jesus states that he's heading to Jerusalem to be mocked, mistreated, tortured, killed, and raised from the dead (Luke 19:31-33)—reminding us that his own death on the cross was God's way of achieving victory as Messiah.

## ENTRY REQUIREMENTS AT THE BEAUTIFUL GATE

In Acts 3:1, the location of the lame man at the Beautiful Gate highlights the apostles' priorities after Pentecost. The details in Acts provide valuable clues to help us navigate our journey to announce Jesus' kingdom.

An inmate reads Acts 3:1, and I briefly introduce Peter and John, describing the temple in Jerusalem as the holiest site for Jews at that time.

"What details do you notice about the characters?" I ask. "Who are they and what are they doing?"

The men observe that Peter and John are going towards the temple at the ninth hour, the hour of prayer. This brief look at the apostles' activities sharply contrasts with the movements of the man born lame. I invite someone to read the next two verses, Acts 3:2-3, "And a man who had been lame from his mother's womb was being carried along, whom they used to set down every day at the gate of the temple which is called Beautiful, in order to beg alms of those who were entering the temple. When he saw Peter and John about to go into the temple, he began asking to receive alms."

"What do we know about this man?" I ask. People mention that he was severely disabled. He had to be carried by others because he couldn't walk himself. He was poor because his disability kept him from working, requiring him to beg for a living.

"Do you know people like this?" I ask. A Mexican farm worker recalls that there are beggars like this in his city, and all over Mexico. Another inmate mentions a friend who was in a car accident and is now a quadriplegic. Others have family members who are bedridden after losing limbs due to advanced diabetes. Someone mentions feeling disabled and lame sitting there in jail, not able to do anything for his family or his case.

"Where is the man and what is he doing when Peter and John encounter him? Is he in church? Is he looking for God?" I ask, inviting people to notice the absence of right-looking religious behavior.

"The lame man is being carried along so he can beg," someone replies.

We notice that he's heading in the same direction as Peter and John. I ask whether he's going inside the temple to pray.

"No, he's outside the temple, where he sits and begs from people going in."

"So Peter and John are heading into the temple to pray to God. Is the beggar looking for God?" I ask to draw further attention to the beggar's position.

Everyone can see that at the "hour of prayer" the lame man remains outside the temple; he is not focused on God at all but has positioned himself perfectly for his most promising opportunity to beg for silver and gold to meet his needs. The lame man is focused on money. When reading this story with people in recovery from addictions to drugs and alcohol, they easily see that the beggar's higher power appears to be silver and gold.

"Where are the places where you work or in any way try to get money?" I ask the men. People talk about their legal and illegal activities, mentioning their jobs, casinos, and even drug-dealing locations. I suggest that, according to this story, God may show up in the midst of their income-pursuing activities, directly or through God's emissaries, to offer them what they really need.

Men and women in jail for drug dealing, burglary, shoplifting, identity theft, and other crimes for illicit gain are always moved by these details. Mexican farm workers, Honduran peasants, construction workers, and the working poor anywhere are equally moved. People are surprised that this lame man's quest for money at the hour of prayer does not disqualify him from God's help, but somehow seems to prepare him to be met and helped in a life-transforming way.

Moreover, the lame man's position outside of official holy sites or prescribed liturgical space or time directly challenges the dominant mindset regarding spiritual pursuit. Most people inside and outside of religious faiths assume God meets people who are pursuing God—through church services in houses of worship, devotional practices, pilgrimages, fasts, retreats, and the like.

Peter and John's encounter with this disabled and impoverished man outside of the holiest place of worship, however, was nothing unusual. Such encounters with outsiders were normal during Jesus' ministry, as we have seen in the story of Jesus' call of Matthew, his healing of the Centurion's servant, his healing of the blind beggar at the entrance to Jericho, and his calling of Zaccheus. Peter and John were direct witnesses of Jesus' many encounters with desperate people outside of the formal religious sites, beginning with their own call on the shores of the Sea of Galilee—which we will see in the next chapter.

Let's turn now to Peter and John's own training with Jesus. How did Jesus prepare them to step into his mission after Pentecost? Let's take careful note of what they learned from Jesus that carried forward into their ministry after his ascension, and can continue to inspire us as we seek to follow Jesus now.

# 2

# Prototype Disciples

## Peter & John, Me & You

Peter and John are inspiring teachers if we're drawn to follow Jesus now. Peter and John inaugurate a way of being agents of healing and holistic transformation that mirrors their master, Jesus. They move from being prototype disciples of Jesus during his earthly life, as described in Luke's Gospel, to a full-on apostolic missionary team in his physical absence as depicted in Acts of the Apostles. As prototype disciples of Jesus, they were prepared to step into Jesus-like mission in the power of the Spirit. Their actions in these two books inspire imitation as they demonstrate holistic transformation. Before exploring the details of their role in the healing of the man lame from birth, let's look at how Luke and Acts present them as archetypal disciples. What can we learn from these early apostles for life and ministry today?

Peter and John's experiences together in several key stories of Luke's Gospel clearly inform their new lives as Jesus' followers after Pentecost. They were among the first disciples whom Jesus called from the seashore in Capernaum. They left their means of sustenance as fishermen in response to Jesus' call, setting out on an adventure of faith. What compelled these first disciples to leave everything and follow Jesus? Let's look at the back-story of their calling before examining more closely what hooked these fishermen. Careful observation of the way people are drawn to Jesus, including Peter and John, can challenge and inspire us too.

Peter is first mentioned under the name Simon in Luke's Gospel, right at the beginning of Jesus' ministry, which started in Simon's hometown, Capernaum. Jesus rebukes "the spirit of an unclean demon" from a man in Capernaum's synagogue on the Sabbath (Luke 4:33-36). "What is this message?" amazed onlookers ask, "For with authority and power he commands the unclean spirits, and they come out." The narrator comments that "the report about him was getting out into every locality in the surrounding district" (Luke 4:37). Undoubtedly, Simon and John got word of Jesus then, too.

In the next scene, Jesus leaves the synagogue and enters Simon's home, where his mother-in-law is suffering from a high fever. Jesus rebukes the fever, it leaves her, and she waits on him (Luke 4:38-39). Jesus then ministers healing and deliverance to the wider community from Simon's house as the sun is setting. "All who had any sick with various diseases brought them to him; and laying his hands on every one of them, he was healing them. And demons also were coming out of many, crying out and saying, 'You are the Son of God!' And rebuking them he would not allow them to speak, because they knew him to be the Christ" (Luke 4:40-41).

Jesus then leaves Simon's house with no mention of encountering him yet. Seeking solitude, with crowds searching for him, he states his wider mission: "I must preach the kingdom of God to the other cities also, for I was sent for this purpose" (Luke 4:43). Jesus then leaves Galilee for a preaching tour through the synagogues of Judea, but returns to Galilee's seashore at Gennesaret, where Simon and John are present, as he teaches on the shore with a crowd pressing around him, listening.

I read this story with groups of working class men in Skagit County Jail and in a nearby prison, Washington State Reformatory, with Spanish-speaking inmates. Before reading the text aloud, I introduce the topic of shame, defining it as the feeling of being irreparably flawed and visibly lacking, like a beat up car with so many problems that is beyond repair. I then ask people whether they can identify with these feelings. "Where do you experience shame?" I ask.

Incarcerated men and women are intimately acquainted with shame. The men talk about being escorted by guards in their red jail-issue uniforms, with leg irons and handcuffs, into court before the judge, the public, prosecutors and other attorneys, and court personnel wearing suits and ties. Their inability to post bail gives them the appearance of being failures, guilty of charges before they even plead.

Someone mentions groups of citizens on official jail tours looking in on them through the glass of their cellblocks. "It's like they're viewing us as animals in a zoo, except worse—because we have obviously failed."

We read Luke 5:1 together, which describes Jesus standing by the Lake of Gennesaret surrounded by a crowd of listeners. The men are intrigued that Jesus is not teaching in an official religious location but outside in nature, at the job site of fishermen at the periphery of Capernaum in Galilee, which is already on the margin of Israel. Jesus goes to where people are, not expecting them to come to him or to religious places.

I am continually inspired by Jesus, who enters the world of ordinary, working-class people. I love how Jesus goes to the margins, Galilee, the Lake of Gennesaret, the other side of the lake, Samaria, and other non-religious places, rather than expecting them to come to him or to religious sites.

Jesus sees two boats lying by the edge of the lake at the jobsite of fishermen. We observe together with the inmates that in contrast to the crowds "pressing around him and listening," the fishermen are washing their nets. We imagine them off to the side, checking out Jesus from a distance, a posture that most everyone I'm reading with can relate to. We soon learn that they hadn't caught anything in spite of toiling all that previous night, making Jesus present in the place of their failure and shame.

Ne xt, Jesus is described as taking the initiative in moving closer to one of the fishermen, Simon. Jesus does this by entering into the heart of his workspace, an empty boat—the site of his most recent failure. I invite someone to read Luke 5:3. "And he got into one of the boats, which was Simon's, and asked him to put out a little way from the land."

"Jesus is rather famous at this point," I mention to the inmates. "He was likely viewed as a kind of celebrity. He had gathered a big crowd of local people. If you were Simon, how would you feel if Jesus publicly got into your boat and asked for your help to push out from the shore there in front of all the people?"

People can see that this would be a big honor—to have Jesus ask you for help, and to be able to use your boat and skills to help him and your community hear him as he teaches. We read on about how he sat down and taught, and then imagine the scene there before the whole crowd. "And when he had finished speaking, he said to Simon, 'Put out into the deep water and let down your nets for a catch.' And Simon answered and said, 'Master, we toiled all night and took nothing! But at your word I will let down the nets'" (Luke 5:3-4 ESV).

Suddenly it dawned on me that Jesus asked Simon to let down his nets before a whole crowd of people.

"How would you feel if you were Simon, being asked by Jesus to put down your nets in front of the entire community who had gathered to hear Jesus, after having worked all night and caught nothing?" I ask the men.

We discuss how Simon has just cleaned his nets after catching nothing, and how Jesus is asking him to get them messed up again, likely for nothing. People mention the potential shame that Simon (and they) could easily feel to fish again after failing, and the utter disgrace they'd experience pulling up empty nets again before the whole community in full daylight—an embarrassing exposure of ineptitude.

Here is one of the places in the Gospels where Jesus makes me particularly uncomfortable, putting me in a kind of crisis or bind. Following Jesus in his miracle working activities has often felt out of my range. Insecurity, fear, unbelief, and pride have often held me back from practicing Jesus' ministry as he practiced it. Asking someone to do something that would require some kind of miracle with the risk of public disappointment or shame if nothing happened is something I can hardly see myself doing.

I am keenly aware of the real and perceived power differential between myself as a Caucasian, American citizen, middle-class, educated professional, and the poor, often illiterate people with whom I work. If some miracle did happen resulting from my word to someone, the prospect of power being attributed to me makes me feel particularly uncomfortable. I desire to see people on the margins empowered, and I am committed to the deliberate relinquishing of power and to intentional downward mobility. I am especially averse to asking someone to do anything that might shame them if they couldn't or wouldn't do it, or to feel pressured to comply in order to somehow pay me back for something or please me.

I discuss with the inmates how saying "no" to Jesus would bring disgrace before the community, and how Simon's calling him "master" (boss) and acquiescence "but at your word, I will let down the nets," could show Simon's accommodating hospitality, or at worst a humiliating submission, even more than authentic faith. Simon lets down his nets, before the onlookers on the shore and us as readers, without any of us knowing his motives. We've only read Luke 5:5, so there's anticipation as I ask someone to read the next verse. "And when they had done this, they enclosed a great quantity of fish; and their nets began to break; and they signaled to their partners in the other boat, for them to come and help them. And they came and filled both of the boats, so that they began to sink" (Luke 5:6-7).

We note together how the text emphasizes that "they" let down the nets, and wonder if "they" includes Jesus and Simon, as there is no one else mentioned as being in the boat. However it looks like "they" refers to Simon and perhaps his assistants, as "they signaled to their partners in the other boat" to help them, though Jesus must have also been there. They fill their boats until they nearly sink, and it looks from the shore like all the credit is going to Simon and his helpers—an aspect of Jesus' healing ministry that we see taken up in Peter and John's later practice. Seeing how these stories unfold alongside people caught up in shame has a very real impact, freeing us all to want to trust, inspiring me towards unselfconscious engagement.

"How would you feel if you were Simon at this point, pulling up this enormous catch before the gathered public and your fellow fishermen?"

"Very encouraged," someone says, and nobody disagrees.

The inmates can see that Simon is experiencing public exaltation and vindication as a fisherman and a human being. Jesus' presence with him and specific instructions empower him in his vocation, making him visibly successful while meeting his subsistence needs. Most importantly, Jesus removes his shame, a critical part of his conversion process that prepares him for his later mission.

I flash back to memories of farm tours that we organized in remote Honduran villages during the 1980s, when fields were in full production. We would walk from plot to plot with groups of farmers who had taken our five-day sustainable farming course. The objective was to see firsthand each farmer's crops, and hear the story of how each one's land was changing by gradually implementing the recommended practices of composting, crop rotation, planting and tilling under green manure crops, terracing, and planting to the contour. Most Honduran farmers had been failing to produce their own corn and beans using traditional slash and burn farming practices inherited from their ancestors, and there was a national crisis in the production of basic grains.

We had first challenged traditional Honduran farming practices by planting our own demonstration farm, under the direction of don Fernando, a third-grade-educated farmer with mastery in intensive hillside agriculture. After terracing our steep mountainside fields and restoring the depleted soil through composting and cover crops, our farm yielded many times better harvests of beans and corn than local farmers had ever seen. First, we offered courses for those wanting to improve their harvests. Then we accompanied farmers interested in experimenting with our techniques to help them try out the methods on a small corner of their land. This began with digging contoured drainage ditches, planting pasture-grass barriers, and continued with planting, cultivating, mulching, and harvesting. We also got involved in helping villagers establish gravity-flow water systems, home gardens, as well as teaching classes on nutrition, preventive health, and first aid.

Tierra Nueva's farm tours brought unprecedented attention to individual farmers, most of whom had never been visited in their fields. After the farmer would briefly tell their story, our group would walk through contoured rows of lush green corn and bushy, heavily laden bean plants, followed by questions and a round of applause. I will never forget the pride and joy that would come over the farmers' faces as their failed parcels were transformed into oases of bounty.

After hiking up steep mountainsides, visiting farm after farm, we would return with the local farmers to the village, where Gracie was meeting with the men's wives, teaching courses on nutrition and other health topics. Women saw the health of their families improve dramatically as they began boiling drinking water, practicing good hygiene, growing more vegetables, and preparing nutritious meals. Malnourished children put on weight, and there was a decrease in dysentery, scabies, and various illnesses. We would time our return from the fields to sample some special nutritious bread which had just been baked. The satisfaction on women's faces as they served us coffee and hot bread makes me think of the fishermen's joy at their abundant catch.

In Honduras we regularly witnessed peasants experience success on their plots and in their homes as a direct result of implementing appropriate technologies and healthier practices that Tierra Nueva was demonstrating and teaching. This directly challenged the traditional explanations, which attributed low yields and malnutrition to God's sovereignty, described by Hondurans as "*la voluntad de Dios*" (the will of God).

We watched people's lack of self-esteem grow from heads hung in shame to newfound dignity as awareness of the root causes of their poverty and ways to address them increased. God became more clearly disassociated from their failures. Villagers living in remote communities used to respond to the question, "What do you do for a living?" with, "I'm nothing but a *campesino* (peasant)." As they steadily improved agricultural production, established gravity-flow water systems in their villages, and their family's health improved we heard more confident replies like , "We are peasants!" ("*Somos campesinos!*").

This change resulted from careful trust-building relationships and hard manual labor—and sometimes pride and an insatiable desire for more were unfortunate outcomes. Implementing Tierra Nueva's new farming techniques required lots of initial effort and careful follow-through. Jesus' way of removing shame in this story challenges me, inspiring me to want to go beyond the beautiful empowerment I've already witnessed into a more fruitful way of working with people.

It is the simplicity and immediacy of Jesus' approach that attracts me. Jesus simply asks Simon to lower his nets in the deep water for a catch. No new technique, simply a call to repeat an ordinary fishing practice. Jesus' words lead to abundant provision followed by a deeper conversion and a whole new life. Jesus' approach sheds light on the inadequacy of our development strategy, inspiring me to draw still closer to him so he can make me become a more effective fisher of people.

In the jail Bible study, everyone present can see how beneficial public affirmation would be for them right there and then. Next we look at Simon's reaction to the amazing catch, and I invite someone to read Luke 5:8-10: "But when Simon Peter saw that, he fell down at Jesus' feet, saying, 'Depart from me, for I am a sinful man, O Lord!' For amazement had seized him and all his companions because of the catch of fish which they had taken;

and so also James and John, sons of Zebedee, who were partners with Simon."

Here we have the first mention of Simon being called Peter, right at the moment when he saw the abundant catch, and he falls down at Jesus' feet, expressing his unworthiness. We are getting to know him better as we hear his full name.

"But why does he tell Jesus to go away from him, saying 'for I am a sinful man?'" I ask. The men respond that Simon Peter was feeling unworthy of such a big blessing. We discuss how he may have been afraid of his sudden success, and the men can all relate to this.

"When you succeed in front of everyone, you're set up for a bigger fall. It's better to stay down than to have visible success and then relapse or reoffend and lose everything," a man states. Many of the men are in visible agreement.

I suggest to the inmates that Simon Peter was possibly known in the community as a notorious sinner. We talk about how maybe Simon Peter knows that everyone watching him from the shore is aware of his dark side, that he's doing something illegal, like the equivalent of operating a meth lab on the outskirts of town, or that he's suspected of stealing car stereos or burglarizing houses to feed his drug habit, has done time for domestic violence, or is a felon. Maybe Simon Peter can't handle Jesus publically blessing him in his "sinful man" state, and knows that his neighbors are probably not excited for him. Does Jesus know whom he is blessing? I invite someone to read on to see how Jesus reacts to Simon's plea for him to go away.

Jesus does not leave Simon as he requests. Rather, Jesus perceives that fear underlies his reaction. "And Jesus said to Simon, 'do not fear, from now on you will be catching men'" (Luke 5:10).

We discuss how Jesus addresses Simon's (and our) fear of success, of failure, or shame's return—whatever fear he might have, or we might have. Rather than being put off by Simon Peter's confession, and leaving him more shamed than ever before the public and his colleagues, we notice that Jesus further elevates him by giving him a public promotion: "From now on you will be catching men."

One day, back in Honduras after our initial three years of success training Honduran *campesinos* who had established their own demonstration farms as agricultural trainers,[1] we were asked to lead a Bible study. Reading and discussing Gospel passages about Jesus began to eclipse my teaching on farming. As we sent Honduran pairs out into remote villages to teach intensive hillside agricultural practices, I found myself increasingly drawn to Jesus' way of being, teaching, and interacting. I watched some of the poorest people become attracted to this Jesus who blesses and calls sinners. Simultaneously, as a growing number of farmers were experiencing increasing yields, interest was growing in learning about Jesus. We were being wooed into other dimensions of transformation.

I summarize with the inmates something I'd discovered with Honduran peasants many times in studying the Bible in cornfields, under mango trees, and in people's humble adobe homes. There in the boat, through Jesus' personal involvement in Simon's enormous catch of fish, Jesus catches Simon Peter, James, and John! These fishermen are won over by Jesus' shame-removing ministry. They say "yes" to his full-on inclusion of them in spite of any perceived unworthiness. Listening to Jesus and following his commands leads to breakthroughs in the fishermen's personal and public lives. Public exaltation in turn leads to confession of sin, acceptance of Jesus' embrace, and leaving behind life as usual in favor of following him as evangelists-in-training. "And when they had brought their boats to land, they left everything and followed him" (Luke 5:11).

The men in the jail Bible studies and people in our Tierra Nueva community can see why these fishermen were attracted to Jesus, and are themselves drawn to him. We summarize Jesus' recruitment strategy as a way to remind ourselves what to look for as we seek to identify or anticipate his fishing for us now.

---

1. *Promotores agricolas.*

We note that Jesus takes the initiative, going to the margins of the margins—to the workplace on the shore of the Lake of Genesaret in Galilee. Then Jesus continues to take the initiative, stepping into someone's workspace, which is a place of failure (Simon's empty boat). Jesus approaches Simon, needing his boat and asking for his assistance. Next, Jesus asks his recruit to do something public that is difficult to refuse, inviting risky obedience that leads to public elevation and empowerment in his vocation. Jesus responds to pushback (Simon's feelings of unworthiness), addressing underlying fear, and inviting him into something bigger ("from now on you will be catching men"). Jesus' recruits leave everything to follow him.

Jesus' style of fishing has drawn me into his irresistible net yet again, even as it caught Simon and John. I witness this Gospel story come alive in ways that hook inmates and people in our Tierra Nueva church. We pray together that our eyes would be opened to notice Jesus' presence with us in our places of shame. May the Holy Spirit open our ears to hear Jesus' shame-erasing words and follow him into a life of adventure as his disciples. May we learn how to be agents of healing and recruiting in the places of failure in our world alongside Jesus.

## WITNESSING TRANSFORMING ACTION ALONGSIDE JESUS

The next time Peter and John are together in Luke's Gospel is when Jesus raises the synagogue official Jairus' twelve-year-old daughter (Luke 8:49-56). The story opens with Jairus, a synagogue official, who falls at Jesus' feet, publically petitioning him to come to his house to heal his only daughter, who is dying. The crowds are pressing in on Jesus as he goes towards the official's house. It is then that a woman who has been hemorrhaging for twelve years secretly approaches him and touches him, immediately receiving her healing.

In reading this story with people on the margins, I regularly ask people if there are things about their identity or their prayer requests that would keep them from publically asking Jesus for healing, like the synagogue official did. People mention things like being a sex offender, addict, or needing healing for herpes or another sexually transmitted disease (STD). The woman's success in secretly coming to Jesus makes room for them in their desire to seek his help privately, so as to avoid shame.

Jesus stops and asks: "Who is the one who touched me?" He notices that power went out from him towards someone in need. And yet Jesus does not require the woman to make herself known. Of her own accord, she "came trembling and fell at his feet" to publically tell why she'd touched him, and that she'd been immediately healed.

People are deeply moved that the woman's falling at Jesus' feet is not a requirement to obtain healing, but a response to healing she has already freely received from Jesus. Jesus publically honors her at the moment of her vulnerability to shame by calling her "daughter," covering her as a protective father in a way that she needed then and there. Jesus publically advocates for her, removes her shame, and empowers her by giving her the credit for her healing: "Your faith has made you well, go in peace" (Luke 8:49). The disciples witness the power of Jesus' purity overcoming the woman's uncleanness, causing her bleeding to stop. While this miracle is not so visible, we as readers are privy to the final outcome, and in the next event a much bigger adversary is visibly overcome.

Meanwhile, as Jesus was delayed in stopping for the women he healed of the blood flow, word is sent to Jairus that his daughter has just died: "Your daughter has died; do not trouble the Teacher anymore." Jesus responds by taking attention off of himself and placing it on Jairus, in his characteristically empowering way: "Do not be afraid any longer," he tells him. "Only believe, and she shall be made well" (Luke 8:51). Jairus and Jesus' disciples are invited to step away from fear that it is too late for Jesus to make a difference. They are summoned into total faith that even a dead loved one can recover.

Jesus arrives at the house, only allowing Peter, John, James, and the girl's parents into the room. Jesus models a quiet confidence here in the face of death, and tells the mourners, "Stop weeping, for she has not died, but is asleep." They laugh in unbelief. In minimizing the gravity of the girl's condition, Jesus simultaneously minimizes the importance of his own intervention. Jesus then models his very personal, physical, and empowering approach.

"He took her by the hand and called, saying, 'Child, arise!'" (Luke 8:54). In taking the girl by the hand, Jesus demonstrates hands-on, faith-filled action. Jesus crosses over a boundary by taking hold of the dead girl's hand, overcoming her perceived uncleanness with the power of his contagious holiness, as in the previous stories of the healing of the leper and the woman who was hemorrhaging. Jesus speaks to the girl, showing his belief in her capacity, expecting her to respond and get up by her own volition—which she does. "And her spirit returned, and she rose immediately; and he gave orders for something to be given her to eat" (Luke 8:56).

Peter, John, and James witness Jesus' authority to restore life and empower someone already dead, preparing them for their own later apostolic authority over sickness, adversity, and death. Once again, I feel pushed by Jesus into discomfort as I doubt my courage to move in Jesus-like authority. At the same time, I see Jesus' awareness and care for the girl's immediate need for food, and his response to their amazement by ordering them to tell no one—aspects of the story I am much more comfortable with. But Jesus doesn't let the disciples or us fall back into our theological camps, ministering only within our comfort zones. Rather, Jesus models a way of living constantly open to interruptions by people deemed irreparable, at innumerable *beautiful gate* equivalents, moving in spiritual authority to cross people over into new life.

## EMPOWERMENT, AUTHORITY, AND IDENTITY IN JESUS

Jesus calls Peter and John, along with the other ten disciples, in the next story, giving them "power and authority over all the demons, and to heal diseases" (Luke 9:1). When the twelve disciples come to Jesus suggesting he send away the hungry crowds who have come to hear him teach about the Kingdom of God and to be healed, he calls them to action: "You give them something to eat" (Luke 9:13). The disciples learn to bring even the most minimal available resources (five loaves and two fish) to Jesus, who is able to multiply them to feed five thousand.

Peter and John are given revelation regarding Jesus' unique identity and authority as God's Christ and Son, and his destiny. Peter responds to Jesus' question, "Who do the multitudes say that I am?" with his confession, "the Christ of God" (Luke 9:20). Jesus warns the disciples of his impending rejection, death, and resurrection before he brings Peter, John, and James up on the mountain to pray (Luke 9:28). There, he is transfigured before their eyes, and God the Father reveals to them Jesus' special importance in comparison to Israel's highest authorities, Moses and Elijah. Peter's first reaction is to attempt to honor Israel's dignitaries (Moses, representing the Torah, and Elijah, the Prophets) as equals with Jesus, suggesting they make a tabernacle for each of them. At that moment, a cloud overshadows them, and a voice declares Jesus' identity, presenting him as their highest authority: "This is my Son, my Chosen One; listen to him!" (Luke 9:35). The transfiguration serves as a key moment of revelation for Peter and John regarding Jesus as God's empowered Son, and their highest master. Jesus then descends the mountain with them, where he immediately casts out an unclean spirit from a severely demonized boy (Luke 9:37-43).

Jesus appoints seventy others in Luke 10:1, sending them out in pairs ahead of him as missionaries: "The harvest is plentiful, but the laborers are few; therefore beseech the Lord of the harvest to send out laborers into His harvest." We will see later in Acts 3 how Peter and John practice Jesus' prescriptions as they minister together as a team.

Peter and John appear together a final time in Luke's account when Jesus sends them into Jerusalem to prepare the Passover (Luke 22:8). They are about to discover that Jesus will give himself to them and to the world as the Passover Lamb (Luke 22:14-20). Jesus sends them ahead of him with detailed instructions about how they will find the upper room, prophesying that upon entering the city, they will meet a man carrying a pitcher of water, who they are to follow into a house where they are to ask for a guest room where Jesus can eat the Passover with his disciples (Luke 22:10-13). They experience the reliability of Jesus' prophetic directions, just as they had when he instructed Simon to let down his nets for a catch. This repeat of directional prophesy became a feature later visible in Peter's own ministry in Acts, in ways that keep this practice alive for all future disciples, ourselves included.

Peter and John do not appear together again in the Gospel of Luke. We read how Peter denies knowing Jesus three times shortly after Jesus' arrest (Luke 22:34, 54, 58, 60). We come upon Peter again as he runs to the tomb, sees the linen wrappings, and is astounded at what had happened (Luke 24:12). Finally, the eleven (including Peter and John) tell Cleopas and the other disciple to whom the resurrected Jesus appeared on the road to Emmaus: "The Lord has really risen, and has appeared to Simon" (Luke 24:34). This is the last we hear of Peter in the Gospels, but he has a prominent place at the beginning of Acts of the Apostles.

Prior to Acts 3, Peter, John, and the other disciples are described as going to the upper room (Acts 1:13), where the text notes: "these all with one mind were continually devoting themselves to prayer, along with the women, and Mary the mother of Jesus, and with his brothers." Peter then exercises leadership, initiating the replacement of Judas with Matthias (Acts 1:15-26).

## EMPOWERMENT BY THE HOLY SPIRIT

The decisive transition from Peter and John as disciples of Jesus to their new level of empowerment comes at Pentecost. The sudden coming of the noise like a violent rushing wind from heaven, followed by the appearing of tongues of fire which distribute themselves on each person gathered, launches them into a new beginning. "And they were all filled with the Holy Spirit and began to speak with other tongues, as the Spirit was giving them utterance" (Acts 2:4).

Here the Holy Spirit enables Peter, John, and the other disciples from backwater Galilee to communicate the mighty deeds of God in the languages of Jews living in Jerusalem "from every nation under heaven" (Acts 2:5). Marginalized people finding their voice and experiencing empowerment are hallmark manifestations of the Holy Spirit.

Peter's new boldness is visible in his articulate response to some of the onlookers' negative judgment that those filled with the Holy Spirit were drunk. He interprets the humble Galilean believers' new capacity to proclaim "the mighty deeds of God" in different languages as a sign that the Spirit had been poured out on all flesh in fulfillment of Joel 2:28-32 (Acts 2:14-21). Peter states that the Spirit enables ordinary people to prophesy, which is what makes communication across all barriers possible.

Peter preaches an extensive sermon, interpreting the coming of the Holy Spirit, confronting his audience as having "nailed [Jesus] to the cross by the hands of godless men and put him to death" (Acts 2:23). Peter proclaims God's raising Jesus from the dead, exalting to his right hand, and making him "both Lord and Christ—this Jesus whom you crucified" (Acts 2:36). In response to his audience being "pierced to the heart," Peter calls them to repentance, to be baptized in the name of Jesus Christ for the forgiveness of sins, and to receive the gift of the Holy Spirit (Acts 2:38). Three thousand people come to faith that day in response to Peter's bold proclamation.

In the aftermath of the Acts 3 story, the Jewish leaders bear witness to Peter and John's new confidence, which hadn't been visible prior to Pentecost, but is clearly linked back to their time with Jesus. "Now as they observed the confidence of Peter and John and understood that they were uneducated and untrained men, they were amazed, and began to recognize them as having been with Jesus" (Acts 4:13).

The empowerment of Jesus' disciples through the pouring out of the Holy Spirit at Pentecost is the critical event that brings Jesus' disciples into his ministry of proclamation and healing as he practiced it. The Spirit enabled Peter and John to move from learner bystanders of Jesus' ministry to empowered agents who carry the gospel of God's Kingdom to the nations. The Spirit enables Peter and John to proclaim Jesus boldly, exercise the gifts of the Spirit, call people to conversion, and inaugurate a new community that embodied the Kingdom of God. Peter and John point the way forward for Jesus' followers today.

## THE CHALLENGE OF HOLY SPIRIT EMPOWERMENT NOW

Jesus' life-transforming mission, and its continuation with the apostles, has continually challenged me, exposing the distance between my faith and that of the first Christians. Jesus and the apostles' acts have exposed the poverty of my own, putting me into a kind of perpetual crisis that has moved into a longing to see and experience more. My thirst eventually drew me to pursue greater understanding and experience of the Holy Spirit through attending a conference that overtly welcomed the Spirit and taught on the gifts of the Spirit.

As I listened to a speaker teach on Jesus' ministry of healing and deliverance, and witnessed firsthand people being healed through hands-on prayer, I decided to accept prayer to receive the Spirit's anointing for healing and the gifts of the Spirit. I stood in a long line at the back of the church as a prayer minister and his "catcher" began making their way down my row. I watched nervously as one person after another fell backwards, into the arms of the catcher, after receiving prayer. I was wary of these kinds of charismatic manifestations, and of being "slain in the Spirit." I struggled to keep my focus on Jesus by reciting the Jesus prayer: "Jesus Christ, Son of God, have mercy on me a sinner." When the prayer minister got to me, he put his hand up near my forehead, and without touching me he began to prophesy.

"I see you in a circle of men in red uniforms sitting on blue plastic chairs. I think they're prisoners," he started, shocking me by the accuracy of the image describing my weekly jail Bible studies without having ever met me or knowing anything about me.

"I hear the Father saying, 'I love how you love my prisoners,'" he continued, affirming the ministry practice I'd engaged in already for twenty years.

"I hear God the Father saying he is going to give you fresh revelation from Scripture that will make your heart and their hearts burn," he said. This was a reference to my favorite New Testament scripture in which the disciples describe their hearts burning as the just resurrected Jesus opens the Scriptures to them as they are on the road to Emmaus (Luke 24:13-32). The young prayer minister went on. "I hear God saying that now he is going to anoint you to pray for people's healing, so that your words will be confirmed by the signs that follow."

At this point, I could no longer stand, and fell backwards, overcome by the Spirit. I lay on the ground, my hands burning, troubled and resisting the idea that I would pray for healing. As a white American privileged male working among undocumented immigrants and inmates, I was not interested in power that would further differentiate me from them, empowering me over them in a way that reinforced already existing power differences.

Yet, over the course of this four-day conference, I continued to receive prayer in unprecedented ways as ministry team members and different leaders laid hands on me to be further filled with the Holy Spirit. On the last day of the conference, the main leader, John Arnott, laid his hands on me and blew over me, stating, "Receive the anointing of the Holy Spirit for healing, deliverance, preaching, and mission."

Upon returning home, I found myself thirsty for more of the Holy Spirit, and longing for greater closeness to Jesus. I felt compelled to pray, worship, and understand what was happening to me. I very slowly and tentatively began to pray for inmates during weekly jail Bible studies, and witnessed the Holy Spirit touch people in ways I had never seen before. People talked of feeling God's presence, noticing peace, joy, comfort, heat, and physical healing. Inmates began to ask me how they could draw closer to Jesus, surrendering to his love.

Our Tierra Nueva faith community began to slowly change as Gracie and I began teaching about the Holy Spirit and praying for greater empowerment for people who felt called into Jesus' ministry. Our worship became more vibrant, and we began praying for healing on a regular basis. Over the course of the past decade, Tierra Nueva has attracted a new crew of people called to minister to inmates, immigrants, gang members, the homeless, addicts, and others on the margins. We are seeing more people coming to faith and desiring to leave their addictions and lives of crime. Tierra Nueva's Luke 15-inspired mission to seek lost sheep until we find them has led to a growing community of motley "found" sheep, and the need to build a "sheep pen" capable of protecting and nurturing people to a place of health. The image of the early church just after the Spirit's coming at Pentecost was inspiring me afresh. The dynamic missional community in Acts was an immediate fruit of the Holy Spirit's coming and an indispensable launching pad for Peter and John's engagements.

Immediately following Pentecost, and just prior to the healing of the man lame from birth, the new converts are described as "continually devoting themselves to the apostles' teaching and to fellowship, to the breaking of bread" (Acts 2:42). The texts depict these new believers as a missional community marked by the signs and values of Jesus' Kingdom.

> And everyone kept feeling a sense of awe; and many wonders and signs were taking place through the apostles. And all those who had believed were together,

and had all things in common; and they began selling their property and possessions, and were sharing them with all, as anyone might have need. And day by day continuing with one mind in the temple, breaking bread from house to house, they were taking their meals together with gladness and sincerity of heart, praising God and having favor with all the people. And the Lord was adding to their number day by day those who were being saved. (Acts 2:43-47)

Peter and John's movement towards the temple at the hour of prayer in Acts 3:1 is most certainly part of their daily rhythm of "continuing with one mind in the temple" with other believers (Acts 2:46). Let's now look at the next key feature of mission visible as these two original apostles model Jesus' post-Pentecost mission for us all.

# 3

# Empowering Presence

eter and John encounter a man lame from birth at the
Beautiful Gate. They meet this man there where he sits,
begging for alms outside, and on the border of the sacred site. These disciples exemplify their master Jesus' care for
vulnerable people in extreme hardship outside the established
religious places. They begin a relationship with him that leads
to hands-on engagement. Healing and inclusion into the faith
community result, presenting a holistic picture of transformation. Encounter, respectful presence, hands on action, healing in
the power of the Spirit, and inclusion into community all combine beautifully here at the *beautiful gate*. Let's look closer at the
dynamics of their ministry of presence.

## MINISTRY OF PRESENCE

At the beginning of this story, Peter and John embody what ministry practitioners today often call "ministry of presence." Ministry of presence is a way of living out God's unconditional love
and respect by coming alongside people, connecting with them
personally, demonstrating solidarity and tender care through
humbly being with them in the midst of their lives, and engaging
with them based on their felt needs. I think of John 1:14, "The
word became flesh and dwelt among us, full of grace and truth."
Images of Jesus weeping at the tomb of his recently deceased
friend Lazarus (John 11:1-44), or hanging between two thieves

41

on the cross come to mind (Luke 23:33). I think of Mother Theresa sitting with the dying beggars in the streets of Calcutta, washing their wounds, and of Jean Vanier's humble, respectful presence living among people with disabilities, receiving from them as he would from Jesus himself. Ministry of presence may lead to charity, advocacy, direct action, or any number of potential responses. Let's look more closely at how Peter and John approach this man, and how this connection happens.

We know from Acts 2 that Peter and John have recently been filled with the Holy Spirit, and are now active in a dynamic community of new believers. Peter and John carry God's presence as they approach the temple. However, it is the lame man himself who initiates contact in Acts 3:3: "When *he saw* Peter and John about to go into the temple, *he asked* to receive alms" (emphasis mine).

Prejudice regarding beggars combined with the lame man's request for alms cause most readers to assume the lame man's seeing and asking are motivated solely by his personal need. Yet it is the lame man who initiates this encounter leading to this miraculous healing, proclamation of the gospel leading to 5,000 people's conversion, incarceration, and the ensuing momentum of the Jesus movement in Jerusalem and beyond.

## CATALYTIC SEEING AND ENGAGEMENT

Closer reading shows that the verb used for the beggar's seeing, *horaō*, signifies a deeper seeing associated with spiritual revelation, as when Zacharias and the shepherds see angels announcing miraculous births,[1] people recognize Jesus as the Christ or God,[2] or recognize God's presence or intervention.[3] Even though the lame beggar may be oblivious that he is seeing in any special way, the writer of Acts uses language that invites our

---

1. Luke 1:11, 22; 2:15, 17, 20.
2. Luke 2:26, 30; 9:31, 36; 10:24; 21:27; 23:47; 24:34, 39.
3. Luke 9:27; Acts 2:3, 17, 27, 31; 4:21.

deeper contemplation. The term used here for the lame man's asking, *erōtao,* itself often occurs in the Gospels when people are asking Jesus to heal someone,[4] explain,[5] eat or stay with people,[6] or ask the Father for anything in Jesus name.[7] The lame man's asking suggests we are to view Peter and John, and ourselves, as stand-ins for Jesus, who elsewhere tells his disciples: "Truly, truly, I say to you, he who receives whomever I send receives me; and he who receives me receives him who sent me" (John 13:20).

The lame man's seeing and asking activates the disciples' practice of the same ministry of Jesus in his absence. This Kingdom action is also contingent on these first apostles' own spiritual posture. They must see and move in alignment with the Spirit, who brings to remembrance the teaching and practice of Jesus (John 14:26). Yet, without the lame man's seeing and asking, there would be no ensuing story.

The lame man outside the temple sees Peter and John as sources of charity all the same. He asks to receive alms, referring to a gift or charity donation to the needy.[8] Because of the man's severe physical disability, he was completely dependent upon people's help carrying and giving to him for survival, and this required him to beg for living. This implied that he saw himself as a beneficiary, and Peter and John as potential donors capable of offering their financial help. The beggar's notion of help appears to be limited to financial donations, which is normal, considering his extreme need. Yet his mentality does not disqualify him. As the lame man identifies the helpers and asks for assistance, he initiates his transformation and an acceleration of the disciples' mission. This story demonstrates how would-be

4. Mark 7:26; Luke 4:38; 7:3; John 8:7; 9:2; Acts 1:6.

5. Matt. 19:17; Mark 4:10.

6. Luke 7:36; 11:37; John 4:40.

7. John 4:47; 16:23, 26.

8. *Leēmosyne.* See Luke 12:33; Septuagint of Tob. 1:3, 16; 4:7, 16; 12:8; 14:2, 10; Prov. 15:27.

disciples of Jesus must be attentive to people's advances, regardless of perceived motives.

Reading these verses as we've just done sheds light on relationships which at first glance we may have never thought could lead to mutual transformation. Scripture often provides lenses that help us see how God works in our lives now.

## SEARCHING OUR STORY FOR KINGDOM OF GOD CATALYSTS

When Gracie and I first moved to rural Honduras in 1982, many of the poorest local people came by our house, wondering what we might have to give away. We were determined to avoid reinforcing one of the dominant stereotypes: benevolent *gringo* experts coming to save impoverished, ignorant Hondurans. We sought to subvert these perceptions by living as much like the local people as possible: subsisting off our farm, living simply, laboring ourselves rather than hiring locals to wash our clothes or work the land, travelling by foot or horseback, and learning from our peasant colleague don Fernando, who was the true farming expert.

We responded to requests for handouts by saying that the only thing we had to give away was ideas that people could see demonstrated on our farm and learn about though our courses. Yet we insisted that people shouldn't assume our practices were best without testing them out first on their own land. We attempted to build relationships with the people we encountered. This usually involved lots of visiting around cups of sweet Honduran coffee in their home or ours, and trudging up steep mountainsides in tropical heat to visit their plots. We sought to listen to them and embrace them without conditions, supporting them in their hopes through accompanying them however we could.

As our ministry grew, we eventually upgraded from horses to a motorcycle. As we got to know people and see their needs up close, we began selling seeds, Bibles, picks, shovels, sheet metal for grain storage silos, and other farming implements at subsided prices that we allowed people to pay off over time. While our focus was on deliberately combating unhealthy dependency, we could see people had concrete needs that we didn't want to ignore. We raised money in North America to help neighborhoods and villages without running water purchase PVC tubes and cement for gravity-flow water systems, and to help landless peasants buy farmland. However, our focus was always on providing training to help increase production of corn and beans, and to improve health. "Give a person a fish, and you feed him for a day. Teach a person to fish, and you feed him for a lifetime," was a development mantra.

Tierra Nueva's outreach to undocumented immigrants and inmates in Washington State was another matter. Migrant farm workers didn't have land on which to subsist. They were living in a foreign environment, having to pay for everything with minimal income. We visited workers in migrant labor camps after work, seeking to establish trust and build relationships. Immigrants were wary of us, assuming we were in agreement with US immigration laws, and perhaps even wondering if we might in some way be allied with law enforcement. We heard that border patrol agents were using excessive force in their roundups, and detaining people who were permanent residents, or even US citizens.

As a way to serve the people, actively break through the suspicion, and build trust, we started a bilingual newspaper, *New Earth News / Noticias Tierra Nueva*. We regularly published stories documenting Immigration & Naturalization Service (INS) raids, human rights abuses, and information about their legal rights and the laws of the land. We published letters and art from Spanish-speaking inmates in the jail, and a column called *"Como Entraste?"* (How did you enter?)—stories where people we interviewed recounted their harrowing experiences when they crossed illegally into the United States.

We hand-delivered these newspapers from cabin to cabin in the migrant labor camps, and invited people to informational meetings at Tierra Nueva, with pro-bono attorneys onsite to answer people's questions. We opened the Family Support Center, where we helped people fill out applications for housing and jobs, contacted insurance companies if people were involved in car accidents, and accompanied people to court if they had tickets or needed to quash warrants. We kept our emergency clothing closet well stocked, and gave out diapers when we had them. We sought to welcome everyone, and were usually able to respond positively to everybody in some way, including referring them to other agencies (such as food banks).

We led weekly Bible studies, met for one-on-one visits with Spanish-speaking inmates in the local jail, and made contact with their family members to keep them abreast of their detained family member's legal process. We sought out immigration attorneys who were willing to do pro-bono representation, and enlisted them to assist immigrants who were facing deportation. Gracie became certified as a Spanish interpreter at the local hospital, and we both registered as volunteer hospital chaplains. We coordinated with area churches to provide an English-Spanish language-learning program and migrant Bible schools for immigrant children. We set up an Immigration and Naturalization Service (INS) watch group, sending out volunteers to document border patrol enforcement operations so there would be a presence alongside the people during these threatening times.

Being present with people in these and other ways gave us legitimate reasons to visit them and journey alongside them in times of need. We sought to establish relationships with people, and trust was slowly built. Coming alongside vulnerable people often requires silent service and advocacy at their point of felt need over a prolonged period of time. Connecting with people was our goal, and visiting people in their migrant labor camp cabins, apartments, or houses was our forté.

We witnessed widespread abuse of alcohol and drugs, the breakdown of families and alienation between traditional Mexican parents and their kids who often struggled to succeed in public school system. Many of the farm workers' children became involved in gangs, dropped out of school, eventually ending up in juvenile detention or jail. As we developed rapport, people would share increasingly sensitive and personal issues with our growing staff: domestic violence, fears of being arrested for dealing drugs, suspected infidelity, temptations to take their life, and difficult parenting issues.

Inmates in Skagit County Jail were needy and powerless, at the mercy of the courts and people like us who came to lead weekly Bible studies or offer one-on-one visits. We often got involved in people's cases, advocating for defendants before public defenders, prosecutors, and judges.

Chaplaincy, advocacy, and home visitation became the foundation for our larger mission, which eventually included home Bible studies and a Sunday Spanish Bible study, and other worship services in our Tierra Nueva building. We officially considered our accompaniment and advocacy as unconditional, and never accepted payment for our services nor did we require people to engage in Bible study or prayer.

Both in Honduras and in Washington, many individuals saw us and approached us with mixed motives and a wide variety of outcomes. Many years later, I can now see how certain individuals in both places propelled us in mutually beneficial directions, and bore lasting fruit. I can also see some equivalents in my own life to the man lame from birth's catalytic seeing and asking help from Peter and John in Acts 3.

### ANGEL DAVID

Angel David Calix ("David") is Tierra Nueva's Honduran leader today. He describes his life in 1983 as a twenty-five-year-old *campesino* resembling the man born lame.

"I was stuck in a cycle of poverty, locked up in a system of farming and life with no way out," says David.

David had been farming using traditional slash and burn farming practices that produced increasingly low yields.

"The only solution I could see was working for a boss who would pay me a daily salary ($2.00 at that time)," he recounts.

David describes regularly walking between his village of Mal Paso and the larger town of Minas de Oro along a trail that allowed him to observe our fields from a distance. David reminisces:

> One day I deliberately walked the road right beside your garden and fields to look at the crops. The tomatoes, beans, and corn plants were so beautiful. I felt the need to have beans, tomatoes, and corn like these. I knew that this land had been impoverished. Could their success be because they have dollars? Many of us thought that these gringos had dollars to give us, or at least fertilizer. I had a plan to talk with them, but I was embarrassed. How could I meet them? I had a desire to ask them about how they grew their crops but I didn't feel capable. I thought you all were like the local rich people who keep their knowledge a secret, closed in behind walls.

The following year, don Fernando and I went to the mayor's office to request a letter of introduction to visit several villages to talk with farmers. We had developed a training course for impoverished subsistence farmers that we called "Appropriate Technology for the Use and Management of Steeply-inclined Land." We went to Mal Paso, and David remembers coming to the meeting.

"I went to the meeting and saw that these were the very people with the crops whom I had wanted to talk with. At that point, four of us began meeting with you every Wednesday in Mal Paso," recounts David.

Every Wednesday, Gracie and I rode our Yamaha 250 motorcycle over heavily rutted roads to Mal Paso. Anyone interested would meet at Teodoro's house for coffee. We would then visit farmers in their fields, marking off contoured drainage ditches, demonstrating how to compost, or surveying their crops—depending on the season. Gracie met with the women to cook up a new recipe and talk about health. After a few years, the people began asking us questions about God so we included a reading from Scripture followed by a discussion.

The group grew in numbers, and the men formed an agricultural committee. David advocated for us to provide a loan for sheet metal so Mal Paso's committee could organize a grain-storage cooperative, and we agreed. Later he suggested we help the committee's landless members by purchasing some land for a collective plot, which we did. David proposed we assist the village with PVC pipes and cement for a water system (with the villagers providing all the labor for installation), and we helped them with that too.

David had a contagious joy and was a natural leader. I was drawn to him and began visiting him more regularly in his field and home. David's crops flourished and his leadership gifts became increasingly evident. He became one of Tierra Nueva's first *promotores agricolas* (farming trainers), and eventually the leader of a group of fifteen other trainers who led the ministry after our departure in 1989. He was a master at diffusing conflict and bridging differences between Catholics, Evangelicals, and those not associated with organized churches. Currently, David serves as pastor and overseer of Tierra Nueva, which includes a coffee farm, *hogares en transformacion* (households in transformation), and a growing church in Mal Paso. I visit him annually, and talk with him by phone several times a week to debrief situations, discuss ministry plans, pray, and catch up as friends.

## CEZAR

I first met Cezar in 1995 when he was a twenty-two-year-old gang banger locked up in Skagit County Jail for cocaine possession. Cezar was a scrappy son of a Mexican immigrant mother. He never knew his biological father. Cezar grew up on the streets of northern California, getting involved in gangs and drug dealing at a young age. He sported a vast array of jail-issue tattoos. His suspicious eyes could easily ferret out a snitch, expose hidden motives, and detect even the subtlest breach of trust. Cezar had done numerous stints in jail in California, and was hiding out in Washington from the police for his involvement in a drive-by shooting.

"I was stuck in a circle of drugs and gang life that I never thought I could get out of," says Cezar.

Bobby, an inmate who boasted of more single arrests than anyone in Skagit County's history, invited Cezar to my Spanish Bible study.

"I decided to go so I could pass contraband to other inmates," says Cezar, who found ways to continue drug dealing even while locked up.

"When I saw you, the first thing I thought to myself was that this guy, like everyone who comes into the jail to lead Bible studies, AA meetings, or whatever, was gathering information from the inmates about gangs and drug dealing to give to the sheriff. I was paranoid because of what I was doing in there. I didn't trust you at first until you started visiting me, having one on one's, visiting me on the outside, and not judging me," recounts Cezar.

I, on the other hand, was drawn to Cezar from the start. I loved his endearing smile, quick wit, and brilliant insights into Scripture. Cezar had a charm that drew me in, and his first big request surprises me still. One night during the Bible study, I had asked him where he got the thread to make the elaborate woven hearts and crosses he wore. Cezar pointed to his jail-issue underwear and socks, whispering that they got the thread by unraveling them. He looked at my socks and told me that he could really use the colored thread to make more crosses.

"I remember you took off your socks, and then you gave them to me, and I put them on," says Cezar. "Then I knew you were my friend and I could trust from that moment on."

Cezar invited me to his apartment, where he sold crack cocaine, to read the Bible with him and his girlfriend. After reading the story of the Apostle Paul's conversion, he remembers God telling him, "If I can change and use Paul, who was watching when they were stoning Stephen, I can change and use you." But

Cezar wasn't ready to surrender to Jesus. I met regularly with Cezar, his girlfriend, and their children, helping them sort out their relationship struggles, offering them assistance though our Family Support Center. He called me Pastor Robert, and began phoning me or coming to my home whenever he was in a fight with his girlfriend. In spite of my best efforts at relationship counseling, conflict increased. Fighting led to a restraining order and break up. Cezar took off for California to stay clear of more trouble in Washington.

Eventually Cezar was arrested again and incarcerated in California for a few years for the drive-by. Once released, he moved to the Mexican border to rejoin his mom and stepdad. There he got involved as a *coyote* in his stepdad's trafficking operation, crossing undocumented immigrants from Mexico through the desert into the USA, and drug dealing. I kept in contact with him for a number of years, welcoming him back to Washington State to recover from a stabbing by rival *coyotes*. I loved Cezar, regularly prayed for him, and called him often over a period of fifteen years, hoping and waiting for a miracle.

Then, in March 2012, in a US border town, Cezar was identified as an enemy gang member by a rival gang, and he was signaled out to be killed.

"I was planning on attacking the rival gang, and I was waiting for the homeboys to come for a meeting," Cezar tells me.

> At that time I had a $200.00 a day meth habit. I was sitting there with a bunch of guns on a table in front of me, smoking meth. I was thinking to myself, "What's going to happen when we retaliate since we're outnumbered? Is my life going to end?" Then I heard a voice like a command that was firm with authority, but gentle at the same time. It said: "Surrender to me and go to Pastor Robert." I thought, "What the heck? Is this because I'm high?" I closed my eyes to focus, and that's when I saw your face. I called my family to pick me up and put me on a Greyhound bus for Seattle. Once on the Greyhound, it was like I was in a trance and someone was taking me. When you picked me up and I saw

your face, it was a déjà vu. You were older and had changed since I hadn't seen you in so many years—but you were exactly like you looked when I saw you in the vision. It was like I was blind on the bus, like Paul after he met Jesus, and you were Ananias. You prayed for me and it was like the scales came off my eyes.

We welcomed Cezar to stay with us and he slept on the couch. We baptized him five days after he arrived, and I began meeting and praying with him regularly. He now leads a morning group that reads the Gospels, and a nightly group that reads the Psalms and prays together. He serves in the Family Support Center two days a week, and visits migrant farm worker families in area migrant camps and apartments.

"My calling is to reach out to people who are like me and tell them that Jesus loves them," says Cezar. "If he can change me, he can change you."

## STEPS TOWARDS TRANSFORMING ENCOUNTERS

Looking closely at how the lame man's seeing and asking initiated a relationship leading to holistic liberation can alert us to the beginnings of important relationships now. Peter and John model alertness to the way the Holy Spirit leads that inspires us to anticipate this kind of action in our own lives.

Peter and John encounter the lame man where he sits, in a public setting, while they are en route elsewhere. They do not avoid the lame beggar who is seeking a handout. They demonstrate flexibility in letting themselves be interrupted from their agenda to pray in the temple at the 'hour of prayer.' They do not preach to the man, but immediately engage with him in response to his request for alms. They honor his initiative by stopping and deliberately establishing a connection with the man. At the same time, Peter and John's next actions are perplexing, challenging, and at first glance even disturbing.

Peter and John appear to be viewed by the beggar as healthy and mobile "haves," potential helpers possessing resources and power. Peter and John's way of engaging seems aggressive and off-putting.

## MORE CHALLENGES BEYOND ORDINARY SEEING

"But Peter, along with John, fixed his gaze on him and said, 'Look at us!'" (Acts 3:4).

At first glance, Peter's gaze could be interpreted as a power play. Telling someone in a weaker, dependent position, "Look at me!" could make that person feel intimidated or humiliated, depending on the facial expression, gesture, and tone of voice. Any attempt to practice this must be sensitive to cultural, racial, and social class dynamics. The lame man might assume Peter's command for attention will be followed by a requirement before a handout. If we assume the best about Peter's gaze and request, we can see that he could be disrupting the man's sense of anonymity, breaking the "us-them" separation. Does he desire a human connection with this man who is looking at him as a source of money? Is he noticing this man as someone he seeks to have a relationship with? A closer look at the biblical language may help us (or further challenge us).

The verb here translated "fixed his gaze," as when "Peter fixed his gaze on him," is *atenizō*, which signifies intensive looking, as in to fasten one's eyes, or behold earnestly.[9] It also indicates a prophetic seeing of something that God is revealing.[10] Peter's fix-

9. It occurs twice in Luke and ten times in Acts, in most cases meaning an attentive noticing of an individual. First, in Luke 4:20, Jesus' compatriots fix their eyes on Jesus in his hometown synagogue after he read Isaiah 61 to them. A servant girl later fixes her eyes on Peter, identifying him as having been with Jesus (Luke 22:56). Disciples gaze intently at the sky as Jesus ascends (Acts 1:10). The crowd gazes intently at Peter and John after the lame man is healed (Acts 3:12).

10. As when Jewish leaders gaze on Stephen, seeing his face as the face of an angel (Acts 6:15), or when Stephen looks into heaven and sees Jesus at the right hand of the Father (Acts 7:55). Cornelius fixes his eyes on an angel in a vision (Acts 10:4) and Peter fixes his gaze on Ananias, seeing his deception (Acts 13:9). Paul fixes his eyes on a man lame from birth, seeing he had faith to be made well (Acts 14:9).

ing his gaze is best understood as showing that he considers this poor man of great importance and value as an individual, in full alignment with God's signaling him out. Peter's imperative, "Look at us!" suggests his desire for an authentic reciprocal connection.

Peter's command to the man, "Look at us!" makes use of another Greek verb, *blepō*, whose primary meaning is physically seeing what's in front of you.[11] Peter invites the man to take note of himself and John there before him. Once Peter had the man's full attention, he could divert that attention off the two of them as normal donors and onto someone else—namely Jesus.

The lame man, however, appears to interpret Peter's invitation to look at them as a successful move in the direction of a handout. But the text itself is more subtle. "And he *began* to give them his attention, expecting to receive something from them" (Acts 3:5).

We might assume this man is still oriented towards money, possibly revealing our own prejudices. Yet the text does not state this, and there is no judgment of the lame man. Rather, he is described as expecting to receive "something." Peter's eye-to-eye connection appears to inspire hope in the man. However, the ministry workers Peter and John themselves are not the focus, but the "something." Might the lame man be expecting to receive something other than money? And could this expectation be interpreted as some kind of faith? At any rate, the word here, *prosdokaō*, is used in Luke and Acts to describe anticipating or waiting expectantly, even for the Christ's coming.[12]

It can be challenging to interpret how someone is looking at you, with what sort of expectation. Discernment is needed to know how to address someone expecting direct aid, especially

11. The term Peter uses here, *blepō*, means to look at (literally or figuratively), behold, beware, lie, look (on, to), perceive, regard, see, sight, take heed. It contrasts with the more common term for see used to describe the lame man's originally seeing of them, *horaō*: to stare at, to attend to, behold, perceive, see, take heed. *Blepō* in Luke seems to imply a deeper, more attentive taking notice (Luke 7:44; 8:10, 16, 18; 10:23; 11:33; 21:8, 30; 24:12; Acts 1:9; 2:33; 4:14; 8:6; 12:9; 13:40; 28:26).

12. Luke 1:21; 3:15; 7:19; 8:40; 12:46; Acts 10:24; 27:33; 28:6.

when what you have to offer is less than what the other is asking for, and also when you know that far more is available for someone than what they could imagine.

## I DON'T HAVE SILVER OR GOLD . . .

At this point, Peter speaks boldly and directly to the lame man, responding clearly to his request by naming the desired object without hesitation, "I do not possess silver and gold" (Acts 3:6), before presenting his counter offer. Peter's lack of silver and gold suggests that these two apostles are ministering in alignment with Jesus' instructions to missionaries. In Luke 10:1, Jesus appoints seventy others beside the twelve disciples, "and sent them in pairs ahead of him to every city and place where he himself was going to come." Jesus sends his seventy in pairs to outsiders.[13]

"The harvest is plentiful, but the laborers are few," Jesus declares, "Therefore beseech the Lord of the harvest to send out laborers into His harvest. Go; behold, I send you out as lambs in the midst of wolves" (Luke 10:2-3). Jesus directs them to find the person of peace with whom they are to stay, receiving his hospitality (Luke 10:6-7).

Jesus sends them out empty-handed, stating specifically, "Carry no money belt, no bag, no shoes; and greet no one on the way" (Luke 10:4). Peter and John are consequently not carrying cash. They possess the Kingdom of God as their sustenance, which Jesus promises to those who are poor. "Blessed are you who are poor, *for yours is* the kingdom of God" (Luke 6:20, emphasis mine).[14] This present tense reality of God's Kingdom is

---

13. This contrasts with Moses, who is told by the Lord to gather seventy elders in the tent of meeting upon whom the Lord places his Spirit so they can bear the burden of the people with Moses (Num 11:16-17).

14. They are informed by Jesus' teaching in Luke 16:13, "No servant can serve two masters; for either he will hate the one, and love the other, or else he will hold to one, and despise the other. You cannot serve God and mammon."

what they have to offer. There at the *beautiful gate*, money is of no use, as they have stepped into the realm of God's transforming presence and the economy of God's Kingdom. Peter and John have been "rescued from the authority of darkness and transferred into the Kingdom of the Son of the Father's love" (Col. 1:12). They possess the anointing of the Spirit upon them to act as Jesus' emissaries. Their currency is faith in Jesus' name to speak words of life.

Peter and John are moving towards God's house, and outside the temple gate they encounter a man who receives them there in his "house" (i.e., the place where he sits and begs). Having gone out without a money belt, they are equipped solely with Jesus' word: "Heal those in it who are sick, and say to them, 'The kingdom of God has come near to you'" (Luke 10:9).

## BUT WHAT I DO HAVE I GIVE . . .

Peter does not shame the man for looking for silver and gold, but refuses to reinforce dependency on money in favor of empowering the man to walk. "But what I do have I give to you: In the name of Jesus Christ the Nazarene—walk!" (Acts 3:6).

Peter and John's actions here inspire me to go beyond the kind of empowerment and sustainable living we promoted in the past. Peter's prophetic gaze and bold call to the lame man to look at him invites me to seek deeper connections with people. I want to become more conscious of how another's seeing and asking may be inspired by the Spirit. Peter's confidence in connecting the lame man's spiritual seeing with his own prophetic seeing propel him towards an outcome only possible through Jesus' intervention. How can this story inspire us into similar momentum now?

## SEEN AND ACKNOWLEDGED

In March 2016, Gracie and I flew to San Francisco to visit friends and speak in a church. From the airport we made our way (like

Peter and John en route to the temple), to the BART (Bay Area Rapid Transit), and took the light rail into the city. Once comfortably seated, I pulled out my laptop and started working on an upcoming talk on reading the Bible for personal and social transformation.

A young man interrupted my thoughts with his loud shouting further up the train, a common occurrence in subways in Paris, where I'd been a few weeks earlier. Vagabond performers often board the metro with a short act, and make rounds with a hat for donations. Homeless people or gypsies regularly beg, sometimes after some kind of speech, which most passengers ignore with earbuds. I was able to tune the voice out to concentrate on my presentation. Other passengers had their faces in newspapers or books. Most had earbuds securely in place to shut out the distracting noises.

The voice was getting louder and increasingly agitated, but very articulate. It broke through my concentration in blasts, disrupting my focus:

"Look at all of you, hiding behind your laptops and newspapers, shutting me out with your ear buds and iPhones. Why can't you just acknowledge me by looking at me? I am not going away, and neither are the 10,000 other homeless people here in San Francisco who suffer on the streets. All of the homeless shelters are filled and I have no place to sleep tonight."

His voice grew shrill and hostile as he made his way down the train towards us. I could feel other passengers' discomfort and annoyance. I found myself wondering for a moment what I'd do if he got right in my face. I even pondered whether he might be the type who could pull out a gun. At this point, I hadn't even looked over at him, but was still buried in my laptop, using my café-sitting skills to tune him out.

"Do you realize how painful it is to be homeless and have people ignore you like you don't even exist?" he continued like a prophet, piercing through my defenses.

"It hurts to be treated like you're invisible. I am a person just like you people. But look, right now not one of you will even look up and make eye contact with me. Can't somebody simply acknowledge my existence?"

Suddenly I felt compelled to close my laptop and respond to him in some way. I got up and made my way over to him as he stood in the closed doorway of the moving train, nearing the end of his tirade. When he stopped, I tapped him on the shoulder and spoke:

"Sir, I want you to know that I am listening to you and am deeply moved by what you are saying. I am sad that you feel so ignored and rejected and can see that you are in a lot of pain. You are getting through to me, and I want to thank you for sharing your feelings."

He looked up, stunned and said: "Whoa, I'm not used to anyone responding to me. Nobody ever does this, man."

"What's your name?" I asked. "Sean," which he pronounced *seen*. I then told him that God sees him all the time and knows his pain. I asked if I could pray a prayer of blessing over him.

"Yeah, you can pray for me," he said. "But would you be willing to help me out with a meal first?" he asked.

"Gladly," I responded, and we agreed to meet at Civic Station, where he said his favorite restaurant was located. Sean excused himself to finish his speech, and I sat down beside Gracie, noticing glances from fellow passengers who looked relieved as he continued in a less agitated voice.

Sean met us as we stepped off the BART, and we followed him out of the station and up the stairs to the street level.

As we walked beside him we noticed that he shuffled along gingerly in oversized, unlaced basketball shoes.

"What's wrong with your feet?" Gracie asked. "Are you in pain?"

He told us that he had severed a tendon, and that both of his feet were messed up from break dancing.

"There's my favorite restaurant," he said, pointing to Burger King across the street. He motioned for us to wait there on the sidewalk for a moment, but I said that we really needed to be on our way soon.

"No, no. Just wait for six seconds," he insisted.

Sean walked into the flow of pedestrians with his right hand out, gently saying, "Excuse me, ma'am. Excuse me, sir," a few times to whoever was before him. We watched as pedestrians avoided him without acknowledging him in any noticeable way, like he was invisible. People consistently skirted him, looking down or in the opposite direction, with expert ignoring.

Sean came back to us and said, "See the attitude that we homeless people have to deal with?" Gracie and I were amazed as we followed him across the street to Burger King.

"We all need to be acknowledged, which is exactly what people are supposed to do towards God," he commented, referring to a scripture that I later located as Proverbs 3:6, "In all your ways acknowledge him, and he will direct your paths."

We waited in line at Burger King and two separate homeless men approached Sean, asking him for something. He ordered, and we sat down on some stairs heading up to a closed off seating area. At this point I asked him if we could pray for him or if he'd prefer to wait until his food came.

"Actually, if you could pray for me before your next meal, instead, that would suit me just fine, if that's okay," he said. "But would you mind if I prayed for the two of you?" he asked.

We accepted his offer, and he put a hand on each of us and began to loudly pray, "Our Father in heaven, mighty God, I believe. But help my unbelief!" He went on praying a long prayer, quieting down as he became increasingly focused. "Lord, bless this couple with a happy marriage and a long life!" were some of his final words before a strong "amen."

As soon as Sean finished his prayer, Gracie said, "It seems wrong that we leave you without praying for your feet. You are in pain. Can't we just pray a short prayer for you?"

Sean resisted for a moment, but then agreed to let us pray. I put my hands on his shoes and we spoke healing to his feet in Jesus' name. We blessed him with God's peace and protection. He was visibly moved. He stood up to get his order, and we headed out together towards our next cable-car-like bus, the Muni (San Francisco Municipal Transportation).

As we crossed the street towards the Muni stop, Gracie asked him whether he was noticing any improvement in his feet. "I won't lie," said Sean. "I do not feel the same as before."

"Well then we must thank God and pray some more," said Gracie as we reached the other side of the street.

We prayed for him, and he received his healing in Jesus' name. At this point, Sean's demeanor changed. He looked awe-struck and we sensed the Holy Spirit deeply touching us all. We said our goodbyes and watched him shuffle off a little faster with what looked like a new lightness in his steps.

As we made our way to the underground Muni stop, we felt a lightness, as it seemed God was directing our path. Sean had inspired, even recruited us to see and acknowledge other individuals, and felt carried along in the flow of God's love.

A tall homeless man selling newspapers showed us where to buy tickets for the Muni. We noticed that his claw-like fingers were severely twisted and learned he was in a lot of pain from arthritis. He gladly accepted prayer for healing, and we continued our journey to our friends' house, wondering what other adventures this already inspired weekend would hold.

## TWO-BY-TWO IN SKAGIT COUNTY

We often seek to practice Jesus' approach to ministry according to Luke 10 in Tierra Nueva's Family Support Center. One Monday evening, five of us gathered for thirty minutes of prayer before seeking to enter into a contemporary practice of Jesus' mission.

We have witnessed first hand that Jesus' assessment of first century Palestine is true today for Skagit County: "The harvest is plentiful but the workers are few" (Luke 10:2). There is spiritual openness, great need, and longing among ordinary people to engage in some kind of outreach.

Together we gather to thank God for what the Spirit is already doing in our ministry and community, and ask how we can best collaborate. We seek guidance regarding where we should go. We expect God to bring to mind families who need a visit, specific places to go, conditions that need healing, and any other indicator to lookout for—whatever the Holy Spirit wants to show us.

We seek to practice Jesus' protocol in Luke 10:3-4, going out dependent and vulnerable, with nothing to hand out—as guests rather than hosts. Seeking the person of peace is all about identifying collaborators, who become visible through their welcoming of us as Jesus' sent ones. Rather than waiting for people to come to us, we go out with an attitude of attentive openness, ready to receive people's hospitality, looking for receptive hosts.

Usually we visit people in their homes, and are often welcomed to the table or offered soft drinks, bottled water, or even a plate of whatever they are eating. We often end up praying about their concerns, anything from the need for work to physical healing and comfort.

On this particular evening as we were praying together, Gracie gets the impression, "soft like a marshmallow," thinking it was about the condition of someone's heart. The laundromat across the street beside a Mexican grocer also comes to her mind. Our daughter, Anna and Salvio, Tierra Nueva's Family Support Center director, think we should go to the megastore Wal-Mart. Salvio gets a picture in his imagination of a palm tree, and someone else mentions "black hair." The three of us then head out to Wal-Mart, even though I normally boycott it.

Meanwhile, Gracie and another Family Support Center staff member, Paul, head across the street towards the laundromat, but as they pass by the Mexican grocery store, Los Antojitos, they feel they should go in. There, Paul notices a bag of giant heart-shaped marshmallows by the cashier. Standing in front of the heart-shaped marshmallows is a Mexican woman making a purchase. Gracie strikes up a conversation with her. They accompany the woman outside into the cold December wind. After they introduce themselves and briefly describe how we were all asking God how we can bless people, they ask her if she needs prayer.

"Yes I do, but doesn't everyone?" she says in Spanish. Gracie agrees that everyone needs prayer, but tells her, "I think God is highlighting you." She shares how they'd been praying and had gotten the impression of a heart as soft as a marshmallow. At this the woman seems to melt and says that, in fact, she needs prayer for pain and swelling in her leg from deep-veined thrombosis and some other conditions.

The cold wind motivates them to duck into the laundromat, which is empty, and they pray. The woman cries as she tells how she'd been longing for someone to tell her about Jesus and help her understand the Bible. Gracie and Paul invite her to Tierra Nueva's Sunday service.

At that point she invites them to her car and offers them bags of oatmeal and granola from the factory where she works. The following week she began coming to Tierra Nueva's services. We visited her and her family in their home where we celebrated God healing her leg, and prayed for her entire family. Afterwards, she invited us to share a meal: delicious homemade chicken tamales and strawberry *atole* (a sweet pudding-like drink).

This woman truly expresses a soft heart towards God and us. She is longing to go out with us on our Monday night outreaches, which shows us that Jesus' call for disciples to beg the Lord of the harvest for laborers is a prime example of evangelism as recruitment.

That same evening, when Salvio, Anna, and I go into Wal-Mart, I am skeptical about our prospects. However, as we walk down the first main aisle, we run straight into a big tower made up of stacked cases of Corona beer. Atop it is a big plastic palm tree! There, beside the beer tower, is a man with jet-black hair pushing a shopping cart full of hot chili Cheetos.

Salvio and I approach him, telling him about our mission, and he immediately agrees to receive prayer. We learn that he is from India but is living in Vancouver, BC. We pray for him and encourage him. We are amazed by the nearness of Jesus' Kingdom, and that it appears in such unlikely places like at the base of a Corona beer tower at Wal-Mart. We rejoin Gracie and Paul, and truly identify with the joy of the seventy who returned to Jesus to debrief (Luke 10:17-21).

## ERITREAN ENCOUNTERS IN PARIS

While on the Isle of Jersey in September 2015, I had intended to take the ferry with an English friend to St. Malo, France, and drive up the coast of Normandy to Calais. There we planned to visit refugees seeking entrance into the UK who were living in a tent city called "the jungle."

I was deeply moved by the situation of Eritrean refugees, and also others from Somalia, Ethiopia, Syria, and Iraq who are fleeing oppressive regimes and war. I had read about the desperation of people seeking entrance illegally into the UK through the tunnels under the English Channel, and had some contacts with Eritrean Christians there.

However, on the eve of our journey, the way was blocked by stormy seas, and my friend was unable to get away, leading me back to London and on to Paris via train. Little did I know that God would open a door to ministry for Eritreans and other East Africans in a completely unexpected way that would include a growing team of eager collaborator disciples.

Ismahan was then a thirty-year-old woman from Somalia whom I first met when she visited Tierra Nueva six years earlier in 2009. Since she was heading back to Paris, we connected her to a church we are closely linked to there. She attended a conference where I spoke on September 19, 2015. After the training ended late that afternoon, I asked her if she knew any refugees from Eritrea. She told me that she could take me right then to the Chapel metro stop, where we could look for East African refugees who gather there en route to Calais.

Off we went on the metro on what turned out to be a Peter and John-like adventure. While traveling, Ismahan told me about her sixteen-year-old brother, who was kidnapped and was being held for ransom by Islamists while on the perilous journey from Eritrea to Libya, where he had planned to catch a smuggler's boat across the Mediterranean to Italy and on to France. She needed to locate someone who knew how to get money to her brother's captors, but felt unsafe going as a woman alone. She was glad I was available and interested in going with her.

When we arrived by metro at the *Chapel* stop, we headed along sidewalks crowded with African immigrants, and Ismahan began speaking to random people in Somali or Ethiopian, asking where there were Eritreans or other migrants who might be able to help her. An Ethiopian man offered to help us, leading us past a small park to an underpass where suddenly we were face-to-face with four young men from Eritrea.

They told us they arrived that day from Italy and were en route to Calais, and hopefully London. They said they'd crossed over the Mediterranean in a smuggler's boat four days before, and were headed to Calais the next morning.

We asked if any of them were Christians, and learned that two were Christians and two were Muslims. We were told that the youngest one, a pale fifteen-year-old Muslim boy, was coughing up blood. We offered to pray for his healing, and also to help him find medical assistance and a hotel where they could rest. The young men looked exhausted and desperate, and were glad to receive prayer.

As we began to pray, a small group of Somali migrants came around and began to question us.

"What are you doing?" "Who are you?" "Why are you here?" Ismahan warned me that they were all Muslims and that we needed to be careful as the spiritual atmosphere was intensifying.

Ismahan explained to them that I worked with undocumented immigrants who come from Mexico into the United States, and that I am a pastor in a jail and prison. I shook each of their hands and tried to break through the wall of wariness. The men eventually dispersed, leaving us with the four Eritreans and the Ethiopian man, who was taking a special interest in us.

As he sipped from a large can of beer, he whispered to me in broken English, "Would you pray for me too? I am Christian."

I gladly prayed for him, and then noticed that he tossed his can of unfinished beer into a trash bin.

At that point, Ismahan's twenty-five-year-old brother, Nasar, called, and we found him in front of a money wiring service run by Somalis under the overpass. Together we helped the Eritreans with some money for a hotel, gave them some British pounds for their trip to the UK, and prayed a final blessing over them. The Ethiopian man then told us he could take us to where there were other Eritreans, and people who would know how to channel money to free Ismahan and Nasar's brother.

Nasar is clearly wired for outreach, visible in the special care he showed for the Eritreans and kindness towards the Ethiopian man. He moved with ease among the diverse mix of English, French, Somali, and Arabic-speaking immigrants and refugees as we engaged with people from different nations. I knew from talking with Ismahan that Nasar considered himself Muslim and had been closed to Jesus. As we walked, I found myself thinking that Nasar was afraid of Jesus. This thought was so strong that I finally risked a gentle challenge: "You are afraid of Jesus, aren't you?"

Nasar denied being afraid of Jesus, but I pressed in with this impression, telling him that I thought he was afraid, but that Jesus wanted him to know he respects him. This statement got his attention, so I shared with him how I could see that he had a heart full of compassion for refugees and people who suffer, and that united with Jesus he would be able to help people much more. He agreed that he had a big heart for the poor, and seemed moved by what I said. I asked him if I could pray for him, and he agreed. We prayed together in the street before heading off on our next mission.

The Ethiopian man was gesturing for us to follow him through the crowd and to the Metro. "I know where we can find many Eritreans, and people who can help you," he insisted. Off we went, our guide, Nasar, and a new Somali friend of his following close behind Ismahan and I so they could quickly slip through the ticket control doors to avoid buying tickets. We changed trains several times, and after twenty minutes or so we arrived at *Place des Fêtes*. We followed our Ethiopian guide through streets and alleys until we entered an abandoned school building where 100 or so African and Romanian immigrants were gathered in clusters on an old playground.

"This is an unofficial refugee camp," Ismahan told me. "These are all squatters, and this building is condemned," she said.

Our Ethiopian guide led us up some stairs, past big plastic bags full of used clothes that men were rummaging through. We entered a hallway and Ismahan knocked on the first door we came to. A woman opened it a crack and motioned for us to go away. Dread was visible in her eyes. Ismahan apologized, and later told me that this woman had likely been raped, and was feeling threatened in this male-dominated environment.

We passed by open doors that revealed rows of men laid out side-by-side like sardines, with small satchels of minimal belongings beside them. "Are you from Eritrea?" Ismahan asked in Ethiopian, interpreting for me. We entered room after room of migrants—Somalis from Mogadishu, Ethiopians, but no Eritreans. We moved through crowded hallways past men, some of whom looked like they could have once been pirates, soldiers, traffickers, simple laborers, or peasants.

We turned past fresh graffiti and handprints, and went through a doorway into a stairwell, which we ascended, up steps wet with urine. We were assaulted by pungent odors as we climbed to the third floor, making our ways down hallways and into rooms full of Somalis and on to a room where we thought we'd find Eritreans.

"No we are all Afghans," a man said as we peered into a large room full of side-by-side sleeping nests made of old clothing. In the hallways, many men were squatting with earbuds firmly in place, speaking softly into their cell phones.

We made our way up another reeking fight of stairs, through hallways to another door, our Ethiopian guide motioning for us to keep following. This new Ethiopian friend's spiritual thirst seemed to increase as our journey intensified. Numerous times he turned to me, pointed to his heart and said: "Please pray for me."

Finally we reached a room he claimed had Eritreans inside. After a prolonged exchange at the door, we were welcomed inside. A pregnant woman with three young children was sitting to the right, nursing a baby. Three other women with children stood before us, along with a man. We learned that they were Muslims, and that they wanted us to pray for them.

The man told me that they had left everything, thinking that there was something better here. "But there is nothing here for us," he said. Ismahan and I lifted our hands and prayed in English and in French for God's peace over this household, favor, and open doors for them, in Jesus' name. I'm not sure whether what I prayed was translated, but the people were warming to us. I noticed one of the women continued to cough in a way that sounded like bronchitis. I asked the man, with Ismahan's interpreting, if she was his wife. "Yes," he said. We prayed for her healing and she smiled.

We walked down the stairs to the ground floor, and then around to the front of the building, climbing the steps to the first floor, and making our way one more time through halls full of desperate-looking men. I wasn't sure what we were doing, maybe looking for someone who could help Ismahan and Nasar get money to their brother.

It was overwhelming to see these people, traumatized by their journeys from many difficult places. What perils had they survived? What future awaits them? As we left, a man followed us down the street. He told Ismahan and Nasar that this was the first time he had heard his language spoken in several weeks. He said he was lonely and wanted prayer. We all gathered around him and blessed him—a growing company attracted to Jesus' mission of seeking and saving the lost.

Instead of finding Eritrean Christians in Calais, we found and prayed for Eritrean Muslims in Paris, en route to Calais. Instead of ministering together with my English friends, our growing team included Somalis and an Ethiopian. Rather than feeling overwhelmed and paralyzed by the plight of these people I had only known through news articles, I felt moved and mobilized.

Once back home, memories of these scenes haunt me, and I find myself praying for the people in these places of uncertainty and pain. They are like the crowds Jesus describes, who "were distressed and helpless like sheep without a shepherd" (Matt. 9:36). Jesus said to his disciples, "The harvest is plentiful, but the workers are few. Therefore beg the Lord of the harvest to cast out workers into his harvest" (Matt. 9:36-38).

Debriefing our lives in the light of Scripture, and interpreting Scripture in the light of our lives, illuminates both. Peter and John's transforming encounter with the man lame from birth raises the bar for what is possible, enlarging our imaginations and expectations. I feel inspired to experiment more with being led by the Spirit in my everyday encounters with people, to pay greater attention to each person who notices and approaches me, without prejudging their motives. Peter's prophetic regard and bold engagement challenge me out of my comfort zone, inspiring me to ready myself for more action crossing lines in following Jesus. Let us continue our foray into this story in hopes of refining our discernment so we can have new eyes to see and enter Jesus' kingdom.

# 4

# Authority, Faith, and Empowerment

Once Peter and the man born lame connect eye-to-eye, Peter states clearly what he does not have to give, and offers what he is able to give: "I do not possess silver and gold, but what I do have I give to you: In the name of Jesus Christ the Nazarene—walk!" (Acts 3:6). Peter speaks a word that shows both his confidence in Jesus' name and his belief in the man. This word takes the man's attention off Peter and puts it on Jesus. He engages the man's own faith to do the impossible—walk! Peter then contributes his own faith and strength by seizing the man by the right hand and raising him up, modeling both hands-on help and spiritual authority. The man's feet and ankles are immediately strengthened, enabling him to walk, leap, and enter through the *beautiful gate* into the temple, praising God.

Peter and John do not ignore the man's felt need for money. Rather than giving the man what he asks for, temporarily satisfying his request but not addressing the root issue of the man's disability, Peter offers him a solution from beyond the normal material realm. He speaks to the man honestly, stating that he does not own the world's currency and therefore does not have it to give. He does not refuse to give, but offers something invisible he says he has. What is it that he has to give?

Peter and John, fully immersed in the name of Jesus, possess authority to tell the man to walk. Peter's directive to the man, "You walk," requires the man's action. What Peter gives subverts and effectively dismantles the dependency of the man on other people (to carry him, bring him food, give him money, etc.). "In the name of Jesus Christ the Nazarene—walk!" Peter and John speak out their confidence that this man can himself walk, empowered by the name of Jesus, their master.

## FAITH IN THE BENEFICIARY

Peter and John demonstrate public faith in both the name of Jesus Christ and also in the man lame from birth. This is visible in their directive to him to walk. Once during a jail Bible study, I was trying to illustrate the story of the man who had been lying paralyzed for thirty-eight years who Jesus told to "take up his bed and walk." I turned and looked right at a local crack addict and known drug dealer and said: "This would be like me running into you in the street when you're high and just telling you, 'Hey man, just stop smoking crack! You can do it!'—in a way that showed I really believed you could stop—which I do." The man was visibly taken back, saying, "Whoa man, something just happened there! That was really powerful! I feel like I really could just stop." His sudden realization that he was thirty-eight years old further brought the story home to him.

Peter is expressing the same faith God (or Jesus) displays when he calls or commands people. The foundation of this faith rests in God's original creation of humans in God's image and likeness. Accepting God's faith in us as weak human beings empowers us and brings us needed confidence. This is especially powerful news for repeat offenders and people struggling with addictions.

## DIRECT ACTION BY THE RIGHT HAND

Peter does not limit his actions on behalf of the man lame from birth to declarations of lack and an order to walk. He moves from spoken word to deeds that are contextually sensitive and liberating, suggesting that commands to a person who is seriously disempowered require our accompanying action. "And seizing him by the right hand, he raised him up" (Acts 3:7). The verbs used here imply strong, decisive intervention. With his right hand, Peter *seizes* the man (*piazo*), a Greek verb meaning to officially arrest, apprehend, capture, lay hands on[1]— and also includes the action of catching fish (John 21:3, 10). The second verb *he raised him up* (*egeirō*), means to awake, rouse (Luke 11:8; 13:25), and to resurrect from the dead.[2] Reference to the right hand shows that Peter's action is linked directly to his authority as a son at the right hand of the Father.[3]

Throughout Scripture, the right hand refers to God's intervention in the world. God's right hand upholds the psalmist (Ps. 18:35) and is associated with saving strength[4] and favor (Ps. 44:3). God takes hold of his children by their right hand as a sign of his continual presence. "Nevertheless I am continually with you; you have taken hold of my right hand" (Ps. 73:23). God's right hand is associated with empowering his agents: "Let your hand be upon the man of your right hand, upon the son of man whom you made strong for yourself" (Ps. 80:17). According to New Testament theology, we are raised in Christ to occupy the place at the Father's right hand in Christ, the source of our spiritual authority.[5]

## JESUS' DIRECT ACTION ON BEHALF OF THE MAN SUFFERING FROM DROPSY

Peter and John's seizing of this man is reminiscent of Jesus' own action on behalf of a man suffering from dropsy in Luke 14:1-6.

1. John 7:30, 32, 44; 8:20; 10:39; 11:57; Acts 12:4; 2 Cor. 11:32; Rom. 19:20.

2. Luke 7:14, 16, 22; 8:54; 9:7, 22; 20:37; 24:6, 34; Acts 3:15; 10:40; 13:30, 37; 26:8.

3. Mark 16:19; Luke 20:42; 22:69; Acts 2:25, 33-34; 5:31; 7:55; Rom. 8:34; Heb. 1:3; 1 Pet. 3:22.

4. Ps 20:6; 60:5; 98:1; 108:6; 109:31; 110:5.

5. Eph. 1:18-23; 2:6; Col. 3:1.

As disciples of Jesus, they seek to replicate his ministry in new settings, inviting us to do likewise. One evening in Skagit County Jail, this story came alive for me. One of the prisoners reads the first two verses.

"It happened that when he went into the house of one of the leaders of the Pharisees on the Sabbath to eat bread, they were watching him closely. And there in front of him was a man suffering from dropsy" (Luke 14:1-2).

"Where is Jesus, and who is with him?" I ask the inmates, directing their attention to review important details of the story.

"Jesus is in the house of one of the leaders of the Pharisees, and there's a man there with dropsy," someone summarizes. I explain that this disease causes limbs to swell through water retention, as with gout.

"Who are the Pharisees?" someone asks.

"They were a group of religious Jews who were super serious about practicing the law of Moses written in the Old Testament part of the Bible," I answer.

An inmate notices that the Pharisees were watching Jesus. I ask the men if they've been watched and what it's like.

People look exasperated and one of the men points up to the one-way glass on the wall that allows guards from the control room to look in without anyone knowing. In jail, they are all under constant surveillance. Another man tells how he's been in the system for sixteen years. He lists the different facilities by name, "Federal prisons, state prisons, supermax, and the IMU" (i.e., intensive management unit, "the hole," solitary confinement). He says that in spite of being watched, he's gotten away with stabbings, with slashing someone's face with a razor blade, and he himself has been stabbed and slashed. People are starting to get uncomfortable. I move on to another question.

"I've been stabbed too," says an African American man in his late twenties. "And I've done time in prison. When I was stabbed I nearly bled to death." He pulls up his shirt to show a long, jagged knife wound in his chest.

"It cut off a small section of my heart. The fact that I'm still alive after all the blood I lost tells me I'm here for a reason," he adds.

Another man lifts up his shirt to show a long wound down the middle of his chest, apparently from a knife. I ask someone to read the next verse, to get us away from the topic of knives.

"And Jesus answered and spoke to the lawyers and Pharisees, saying, 'Is it lawful to heal on the Sabbath, or not?'" (Luke 14:3).

I notice for the first time that Jesus is not answering anyone's question, but responding to the question implied by their watching by asking them a question of his own.

Jesus puts these law enforcers in a bind. Are they more concerned with the law or with the man suffering from dropsy?

"What do you guys think?" I ask. "In our society, are people viewed as more important than the law, or are laws considered more important than people?"

"People are definitely more important than the law," says the man who described stabbing others, and being himself stabbed and slashed. Someone observes that it seems this man has probably changed for the better since he was in prison. He nods and seems to appreciate the compliment, agreeing that he has changed a lot.

The African American man states that society definitely sees laws as more important then people. He describes how he was arrested because he was wearing a white shirt, and someone had called the police about a peeping Tom who was wearing a white shirt. Another man says he sees people getting charged for all kinds of minor things, insisting that the law is used in excessive and meticulous ways against them.

We read on and notice that the Pharisees did not answer Jesus' question, "Is it lawful to heal on the Sabbath, or not?" The stark contrast between Jesus' action and our penal system becomes apparent.

"But they kept silent. And He took hold of him and healed him, and sent him away" (Luke 14:4).

The Pharisees' silence shows their refusal to make room for mercy. This silence also gives Jesus the space to answer his own question with direct action. "Jesus literally arrests the man," I tell the men. I point out how in the original language of the New Testament, Greek, the verb translated "he took hold of him" also signifies "to seize, take a hold of, or arrest."

I point out that in another similar story in Mark 3, Jesus questions the Pharisees about whether it's legal to heal a man with a withered hand on the Sabbath. When they refuse to answer, he looks around in anger, grieved at their hardness of heart. Jesus shows his faith in the man, telling him: "'Stretch out your hand!' And he stretched it out, and his hand was restored" (Mark 3:5). I retell how Jesus' defense of this man made him an enemy of these authorities, reading the next verse, "The Pharisees went out and immediately began conspiring with the Herodians against him [Jesus], as to how they might destroy him" (Mark 3:6).

Returning to Luke 14, we are now at the point in our Bible study where the liberating message is about to be delivered, emerging like a bloody but joyfully welcomed newborn.

"Here in Luke 14, Jesus seizes (arrests) him in the presence of watching religious law enforcers," I say. "But rather than punishing or incarcerating him, Jesus heals him and sends him away—away from the watching cops. Check this out you guys, the word here for 'send away' (*apolyō*) literally means 'he releases him!'"

"Jesus is not into law enforcing. He's not in agreement with our penal system. Jesus is about arresting people in order to heal them and set them free from the system," I summarize.

The African American man waxes eloquent at this point.

"That's cool, because locking us up, making us do time, doesn't help nobody. Jail time, prison sentences don't heal, don't make us better. We come out worse off."

People's spirits are lifted, and the final verse where Jesus' exposes and silences the law-focusing Pharisees encourages them all the more. Jesus reveals that even the Pharisees are into restorative, saving work that breaks their own rules on the Sabbath if it suited their interests: "And He said to them, 'Which one of you will have a son or an ox fall into a well, and will not immediately pull him out on a Sabbath day?' And they could make no reply to this" (Luke 14:5-6).

Jesus seeks to recruit the Pharisees into his expansive grace, hoping they, like he, will include people like the man suffering from dropsy as one of their own. Jesus-style advocacy is attractive to us all as we imagine the scene in the Pharisee's house, and I search for ways to bring this home even more personally for the men.

My partner Matt and I decide to leave the last minute to pray for the men with the stab wounds. I ask the men who have been stabbed if any of them still feel pain from the wounds. The African American man says he still does. The Caucasian guy who spent sixteen years in prisons says he doesn't have pain, but suffers from PTSD.

I ask permission to go around and lay hands on them, and all are in agreement. We pray for each man, that they would experience the love of Jesus and the restoration of their dignity through his defending and honoring presence. We pray specifically for each man who had been stabbed, for total healing and freedom from pain and trauma. Peace fills the room as the guards pop the door and take the men back to B Pod.

## RAISING THE BAR ON MINISTRY OF PRESENCE

Peter and John embody a ministry of presence that raises the bar for contemporary practice. On the one hand, they meet an individual who is disabled and impoverished, who is not seeking God but begging for money outside of the religious meeting place. They respond to the person's pursuit of their attention by engaging relationally, making eye contact, and inviting deeper connection. They do not give the handout he requests. Rather, they give something invisible. Peter later calls this "faith in his name." They speak to the man, exercising their faith by ordering him to walk, something impossible requiring his faith and action. Peter and John themselves intervene to help, at the risk of becoming the new 'higher power' for the man. They do not hesitate to get personally and physically involved, demonstrating the need in cases of extreme disempowerment for hands-on action that is radical and strong. At the risk of presenting Peter as the savior, the text does not hide his specific and important actions. There are times when intensive physical, intellectual, psychological, or emotional investment are required.

On the other hand, as Peter is seizing the lame man and raising him up, his feet and his ankles are strengthened. Healing, in this case, is not reduced to human intervention, however deliberate and strong. God's action is required, and happens in the midst of human words and works in ways that are humble, almost secret, and easily missed.

In this story, the miraculous healing looks like Peter and John's powerful work, as God's direct action is not overtly visible or mentioned. The text does not say, "and Jesus strengthened his ankles." Rather, the subject of the verb *stereoō* (make strong, solidify, receive strength) is unnamed, awaiting Peter and John, you and I, to bear witness to the One who saves. The story invites us to consider what this might look like here and now in our own lives and ministries.

## THE WOMEN BENT OVER DOUBLE IN BOQUISSO, MOZAMBIQUE

I witnessed firsthand poor African villagers experience the before and after of Jesus' incognito healing and empowerment in the midst of Bible study on Luke 13:10-13 accompanied by hands-on action.[6] The people of the Presbyterian congregation

6. I was involved in a five-day workshop on "Leitura Popular da Bíblia" (street-level Bible reading) with pastors from different mainline and evangelical denominations at the Seminario Unido de Ricatla in Maputo, Mozambique, in 2009. Dutch missionary or course organizer, Hette Domburg,

of Boquisso, Mozambique, formed a tunnel, singing and clapping as we passed through them into the dirt-floored sanctuary. I led them in a dramatic reenactment of Jesus' healing of a woman in the synagogue—a story similar to Acts 3 that most certainly influenced Peter and John.

Acting out this story always makes it come alive. Someone agreed to play the woman bent over double, and another to play Jesus. The rest of us played the crowd. I invited the Mozambican pastor accompanying us to read the first verses in Portuguese and the local language of Tsonga.

"And he was teaching in one of the synagogues on the Sabbath. And behold, there was a woman who for eighteen years had had a sickness caused by a spirit; and she was bent double, and could not straighten up at all" (Luke 13:10-11).

I invite everyone to imagine themselves as this woman by bending over double and walking around silently for the next five minutes. People laugh and chatter as we all hunch over and walk around inside the meeting space. We then gather in a circle and I ask people to describe what they think it would be like to be bent over like that for eighteen years.

The people share their thoughts one after another. They mention feeling humiliated, discouraged, suffering back pain, stomach pain, not being able to look up, not being able to look at people in the eye, being stared at, and judged.

"Are there situations that cause you to feel humiliated? Do you see people here in your village that are like this woman?" I ask.

Someone mentions that they sometimes feel embarrassed by their teetering church with its rusty sheet metal roof, which was inferior to the bigger and fancier churches in the village. Others mention that many suffer from malaria, and some from HIV/AIDS.

I invite everyone to form a circle, and ask the woman playing the woman bend over double to go and stand hunched over

---

invited me and my son Isaac to visit a Presbyterian congregation in the village of Boquisso.

before the person playing Jesus when he calls. I ask the pastor to read the next line describing what Jesus does, and ask the person playing Jesus to themselves speak out to the woman what Jesus says, and do what he does. The pastor reads in Portuguese and Tsonga: "And when Jesus saw her, he called her over and said to her" (Luke 13:12a).

The person playing Jesus speaks out in Tsonga and the pastor translates into Portuguese: "Woman, you are freed from your sickness" (Luke 13:12b).

The pastor continues reading the next line, and the person playing Jesus acts it out. "And he laid his hands upon her; and immediately she was made erect again, and began glorifying God" (Luke 13:13).

I ask if anyone has any pain in their back or stomach, and many of the people say they do. Others say they suffer from regular nightmares.

I propose that we pray for one of the women who was experiencing chronic back and stomach pain at that moment. I ask the woman's permission to lay hands on her back as Jesus did in the story, so we can demonstrate how to pray for her, echoing Jesus' words: "Woman be freed from your sickness." After speaking these words, I ask the woman if she notices any improvement. She says that all the pain left, and looks overjoyed. I'm wondering whether she's stating that she has been healed to not disappoint us, but others ask for prayer right away. Diverting attention away from myself and the other outside visitors, I suggest that the woman who had just been healed pray for the next woman just as we had prayed for her. At first she hesitates but then agrees. The second woman says she, too, experienced total relief from her back and stomach pain.

I suggest that people envision themselves standing before Jesus as they receive prayer from whoever is praying for them—consciously receiving their healing from Jesus as a free gift. This is a radical idea in a culture where traditional healers charge for their services. As those who have already experienced healing pray in turn for the third woman, she suddenly begins dancing and worshipping, overjoyed, as she states excitedly that all of her pain is gone! Through the Mozambican pastor, I instructed all the remaining people to pray for themselves. About twenty people claimed to experience healing immediately.

An older woman named Elsa, who was the closest actual equivalent to the bent over woman Jesus healed in Luke, was not getting relief. Finally, after Hette and Isaac continued to pray, her stomach pain left. By the time we needed to leave she was standing a lot straighter.

The Mozambican Presbyterian pastor says he's shocked by what he witnessed that afternoon. He tells me that there is healing in my Portuguese Bible, and asks me if he could exchange his Bible for mine. I insist that the healing was not in the Bible, but through the name of Jesus and through the laying on hands: mine, the women's, his, or those of any believer. He nods in agreement but he still wants to exchange Bibles. The Holy Spirit is the hidden agent of healing who secretly strengthens ankles, banishes pain, and transmits the love of God—right in the midst of our words and actions, in the name of Jesus.

## A MAN LAME FROM BIRTH IN SIBERIA

Peter and John embody Jesus' very personal and hands-on presence alongside people on the margins. Peter's bold faith to speak to a lame man an empowering command, "In the name of Jesus you walk!" followed by his actively seizing and raising the man up models like practice today. And the Spirit's incognito presence backing up Peter's words and actions invites faith now. We witnessed this first-hand in the healing of a man lame from birth in Siberia.

Our journey to Siberia in March of 2015 began seven years earlier during a jail Bible study in Mount Vernon, Washington, when I met a twenty-one-year-old Russian man named Andrey. God is now raising him up as an evangelist and prophetic voice in far away Siberia.

Andrey grew up in a Russian Pentecostal family that migrated to Washington State when he was twelve years old. In his late teens and early twenties, he got involved in drugs, leading to stints in jail, and eventually a one-year sentence in Skagit County Jail. There, in our weekly Bible studies, his faith in Jesus was re-ignited. I watched him grow in faith and clarity of calling from month to month, and advocated for him during his year in immigration detention.

I have often advocated for immigrants charged with worse crimes than Andrey's and won "cancelation of removal," which allows people to retain their permanent residency status. Winning Andrey's case required the local prosecutor's cooperation. Sadly, he refused in spite of widespread community support.

The best legal counsel, a massive prayer effort on the part of his family and church, and my own testimony as a character witness in his trial before a judge I even knew personally did not stop his removal. In 2010, Andrey was "cast out," perhaps accomplishing Jesus' instructions to evangelizing disciples to "beg the Lord of the harvest to *cast out* (*ekballo*) workers into the harvest" (Luke 10:2). Andrey was deported back to Russia with a lifetime bar from re-entry into the United States.

Andrey and I kept in touch through Facebook, where I learned that he attended a Bible school and became active in a network of churches. A few years ago, Andrey, in coordination with the bishop of the churches he worked with, invited Gracie and I to Russia, believing that our approach to ministry would be helpful there.

When I learned he was located in Siberia, I was reluctant to go due to uncertainty about what we'd be doing, an already busy schedule, lack of funding for the trip, and maybe even some childhood fear. I grew up during the Cold War, when the Soviet Union was America's number one enemy. I remember as a child hearing that if the Russia communists took over America, they would persecute Christians. This would likely include me being separated from my parents, being sent to a re-education camp, or maybe even to a prison labor camp in Siberia. I always wondered whether I would hold up under persecution. This childhood fear may well have contributed to some hidden reluctance, which was soon overcome.

Krasnoyarsk was in the heart of the Soviet Gulag, and reputedly has some forty prisons in the surrounding area. The more Andrey persisted, the more Gracie and I felt we were being called to go—even if the Russian churches couldn't cover our travel costs. A week after buying the tickets with our credit card, a generous donor called us out of the blue and offered to pay for our airfare.

In March, Gracie and I flew from Seattle to Bangkok, then continued via a seven-hour flight over China and Mongolia to frigid Krasnoyarsk. We touched down on a dark, snowy night and minus twenty two-degree temperatures. "What had we gotten ourselves into?" we wondered.

Andrey had organized a packed schedule for our ten days together. He drove us from church to church, through snowy aspen-covered hills and plains on Siberia's permafrost-damaged roads, interpreting for us as we ministered together.

The first day we were to speak at a local conference, and were asked to teach on the broad topic of relationships. "What exactly are you hoping for?" we asked. We were told that people knew almost nothing about relationships with the opposite sex, and needed basic teaching on communications skills, conflict resolution, marriage, and child-raising.

Some sixty people showed up in a large log cabin-like structure heated by coal (the same as every place). In prayer I'd gotten the impression that God wanted to heal people with hepatitis C. After worship, I mentioned this and invited people forward who had this disease. I was shocked to see over half the people come forward, including the five pastors attending the conference. Large numbers of men and women continued to respond to this same invitation in seven different churches.

We learned that most all of the pastors in this denomination, and a large percentage of the congregation, had been heroine addicts, and many had done time in a Siberian prison. The social chaos that ensued right after the fall of the Soviet Union in the early '90s included widespread use of intravenous drugs, and many had contracted hepatitis C.

We were inspired to learn that twenty-five of the thirty-five churches in the network had their own recovery houses, and the denomination ran a yearlong Bible school that most of the pastors had attended immediately after their year in rehab. For two days, we taught the fifty or so students in this Bible school, most of whom had come straight out of recovery houses.

Everywhere we went we prayed for people's healing of hepatitis C and many other conditions. Soon we received report after report of people having experienced either intense heat, pain, or throbbing in their livers when we prayed, followed by the disappearance of symptoms. While we have yet to hear about blood tests confirming healings, we believe Jesus was healing people's livers as we saw others get relief from other chronic conditions as they were also filled with the Holy Spirit.

We witnessed God healing people's hearts and freeing people from demonic oppression during ministry times. The pastors told us about the national problem of fatherlessness due to the approximately thirty million men killed in World War II, in addition to widespread death during Stalin's purges. Many of the people to whom we ministered had been raised by single mothers, or by fathers who themselves had not been fathered, and had suffered blocks to knowing God as Father as a result.

The last two days were the highlight of our trip, as some 250 people gathered for a conference on holistic liberation. On the first day of the conference, during worship, we had noticed a young man whom was profoundly disabled. He was bent over double from cerebral palsy and he dragged his right leg behind him as he walked, hands clasped tightly.

On the last night we were told to not invite people forward for prayer for hepatitis C, because probably 90% of the people had it. Rather, the pastors suggested we have a prayer tunnel formed by the pastors and ourselves.

That night we prayed for hours as men and women filed between us. We were deeply affected by the condition of the people who came through the prayer tunnel. Many had scars on their heads, their bodies wracked by years of neglect and drug abuse. The young man who was lame passed between us, and we laid hands on him, prayed for Jesus to heal him, rebuked the plans of the enemy, and blessed him. However, we didn't notice any visible change in him or in anyone we prayed for that night—though in the middle of the night Gracie found herself praying for his freedom in Jesus' name.

The next day after our final Sunday service, before flying on to South Korea, a woman approached us gushing with enthusiasm. Andrey translated for her as she thanked us for praying for her son. "He is now able to bend his leg and he is standing completely straight!" she exclaimed.

At first we had no idea who she was referring to. Soon we learned from Andrey that the woman's son was the man lame from birth we'd prayed for the night before in the prayer tunnel. The young man was brought to us, and we were able to witness first-hand the dramatic healing he had experienced the previous night. He showed us how he could bend his leg and back as he stood straight, his hands open. We learned that he was born with cerebral palsy, He told us how he had felt the Holy Spirit connect his brain to his leg and was experiencing a restoration of his memory.

It wasn't until the morning that this man's healing was evident, unlike the visibly immediate healing of the man lame from birth, "With a leap he stood upright and began to walk; and he entered the temple with them, walking and leaping and praising God" (Acts 3:8).

Unlike the man lame from birth, this man's healing happened imperceptibly, in the midst of people's hands-on care, or during the night in the privacy of his bedroom. In our story in Acts 3, the man himself appears to be given credit. He responds to Peter's command, "Walk!"

Like the healing of the Siberian man, supernatural healing happens in the mysterious mix of Peter's agency and that of the man. What is perceived from the outside is Peter's seizing of the man and lifting him up to his feet. The work of God is often hidden. Based on observation alone, all the credit could easily go to Peter and John—much as this young man's healing was attributed to us. Ministry of presence combined with supernatural healing has the potential of drawing attention to the ministry workers. It is here that we must turn to the next scene in our story—where we see proclamation of salvation in Jesus' name modeled by the apostolic team.

# 5

# Embracing the Rejected One

## A Theology of the Cross

At the Beautiful Gate, a dramatic miracle has taken place at the threshold of the temple—the Jewish people's most holy place. A man recognized by all as a chronically lame beggar has just been publically embraced, raised up, and healed by Peter and John, leading to his crossing the line into the temple, walking, leaping, and praising God. The man has gone through a transformation from being a crippled, dependent, excluded one begging for money outside the sacred gathering place to a healed, mobile worshipper of God, actively present in the heart of the community that had excluded him. Inside the exclusive sacred space of the temple, before a crowd of onlookers astounded by the miracle, Peter articulates Kingdom of God priorities. How does Peter seize the moment to speak to and challenge the heart of his listeners? What does he show us about prophetic witness and proclamation of good news now?

Peter immediately deflects attention away from himself and John, bolding announcing that the God his Jewish listeners claim to worship fully endorses Jesus who they have recently rejected and killed. Rejection of Jesus as Israel's and the world's Savior is widespread today, though many are finding him irresistible—humanity's holy hope. Yet even Christians are among those who balk at his way of saving through the surrendering of his life to hostile humans, who he deliberately forgives and chooses to love. Christian resistance to Jesus grows as our world becomes increasingly violent and highly polarized. While people may choose him as their eternal Savior, fewer agree to follow him as commander-in-chief of every domain of life here and now. Healing in Jesus' name, prophetic exposure of hostility towards Jesus as God's most total revelation, and call to repentance are all essential to holistic ministry now.

Crossing the line through the *beautiful gate* brings us from the realm of the excluded into the domain of the excluders. The temple represents places where only the qualified are welcomed. Jesus is the excluded victim par excellence, who died "outside the camp" (Heb. 13:13). Peter and John represent Jesus and must speak for him and for the Father who glorifies him. Embracing Jesus, the rejected and crucified, is essential for stepping into his ministry of embracing the excluded. Confessing and repenting of our own tendency to reject, disown, deny, and kill is essential if we're to engage in Jesus' mission (and Peter and John's apostolic mission) outside of today's "temples."

Once inside the *beautiful gate*, new perils and risks must be addressed. These dangers are also present today for both the change agents and the people who directly benefit from Jesus' saving help as they step into mainstream society and even into the community of believers called the church.

Before this miraculous public healing, the Jewish religious public who frequented the temple might have thought nothing had changed as a result of Jesus' short life, recent execution, and reputed resurrection and ascension. Jesus had traveled from village to village in Galilee, Samaria, and Judea, embracing the excluded, healing the sick, casting out demons, and teaching the people. He had engaged with the constant challenges and opposition from Jewish religious leaders. Jesus had even taught and healed there in the temple, and driven out the moneychangers in a dramatic protest against Mammon. Then he was betrayed by one of his own disciples, delivered over to the Jewish religious authorities, abandoned at his arrest by his confidants, turned over to the Roman authorities by his own people, convicted by Pilate, and executed by crucifixion at the hands of the Romans.

Those threatened by Jesus, who instigated his killing, may have assumed they had succeeded in wiping him and his movement out for good. In the aftermath of Jesus' execution, burial, and resurrection reported by his disciples, public religion likely continued as normal, as if Jesus had never come. Jesus was on the way to becoming a forgotten figure, fading into irrelevancy, as the daily grind of the Roman occupation marched relentlessly on. Jesus was clearly less visible and likely more forgotten than the man lame from birth, who himself was a regular reminder to those entering the temple that Jesus hadn't finished his mission.

Not all of the blind had received their sight, not all of the lame were walking, not all the lepers cleansed, nor were all the dead raised. Not all of the poor had the Gospel preached to them. John the Baptist's earlier question to Jesus in Luke 7:20, "Are you the expected one, or should we look for another?" was likely assumed by many to be clearly answered, "No, Jesus was a failed liberator, an irrelevant option, a disappointing mirage, a blasphemous intrusion." Two of Jesus' own disciples had stated their disillusionment to the resurrected Jesus himself before they recognized him on the road to Emmaus: "But we were hoping that it was he who was going to redeem Israel" (Luke 24:19).

Today, too, it is easy to be overwhelmed by the state of the world, the plight of the poor, the incarcerated, the addicted, the mentally ill, the sick, people groups and species threatened by extinction, and countless other concerns. It appears on the surface that little or nothing has changed as a result of Jesus, making this story and Peter's proclamation highly relevant for us now.

These disciples demonstrate that Jesus' ministry has not been snuffed out, but continues. Peter publically displays the invincibility of the resurrected Jesus in the heart of Israel's temple in ways that get people's full attention. Jesus' disciples will make Jesus' victory visible in his physical absence through praying for the sick, casting out demons, and announcing of God's Kingdom in Jesus' name. Without the ongoing embodiment of Jesus' ministry in the temple, there would be no astonished crowd to address. The story also shows that visible signs and wonders were accompanied by overt proclamation giving glory to Jesus, suggesting the importance of like practice now. The content of this proclamation today must directly address each unique context appropriately. Yet, our communication should also be informed by the messages of Jesus' first apostles.

## THE CRUCIFIED MESSIAH REVEALED AT THE PORTICO OF SOLOMON

Prophetic proclamation occurs in the next scene as all the people run to the Portico of Solomon full of amazement, with the lame man now fully healed and clinging to Peter and John (Acts 3:11). This colonnade or cloister, named after King Solomon, located on the eastern side of the temple's outer court (the women's court), is only mentioned one other time in the Bible, John 10:23. Jesus is described as walking in the Portico of Solomon before the Jews gather around him to ask him if he is the Christ. Jesus responds: "I told you, and you do not believe." He then refers to the works that attest to his identity, and challenges his interrogators: "The works that I do in my Father's name, these testify of me. But you do not believe because you are not of my sheep" (John 10:25-26). Jesus says his sheep hear his voice, follow him, receive eternal life, never perish, and are never snatched from his or his Father's hand. "I and the Father are one," says Jesus, provoking the Jews to pick up stones to stone him for blasphemy (John 10:30-31).

In this same Portico of Solomon, before a gathered crowd of amazed onlookers, Peter insists that this Jesus, executed by his adversaries had not faded into history as an irrelevant would-be liberator. The healing of this man born lame, and contemporary versions of this miracle, provide occasions to challenge the status quo with powerful signs that Jesus is alive now. With the man once lame from birth clinging to him, Peter addresses the adulating crowd, taking the attention off of himself and John and re-focusing it onto Jesus. Then he directly addresses people's past history with Jesus, calling them into repentance and reconciliation.

## DEFLECTING AND RE-FOCUSING PUBLIC ATTENTION

"But when Peter saw this, he replied to the people, 'Men of Israel, why are you amazed at this, or why do you gaze at us, as if by our own power or piety we had made him walk?'" (Acts 3:13).[1]

This miraculous healing could have served as a perfect authentication of Peter and John's apostolic authority as a new generation of healers, appealing to people's desire for more miraculous acts of power to overcome the toil, trouble, and sicknesses that afflicted people everywhere. Peter challenges the common assumptions that he and John themselves were powerful, or that the healing was a sign of God's favor due to their superior righteousness. In stark contrast to an emphasis on the dominant notions of power and glory as success due to righteousness, Luke offers his version of a theology of the cross that must be examined in detail and applied to our times.

## PREACHING A THEOLOGY OF THE CROSS TO PERPETRATORS

By theology of the cross,[2] I am referring to an understanding of God's self-revelation in Jesus, his son, as most fully visible in his suffering and death on the cross. Jesus reveals the Father in his self-emptying love for the world, dying for us "while we were yet sinners" (Rom. 5:8). He saves us by grace while we are still his

1. The text also emphasizes that, "all the people saw him walking and praising God; and they were taking note of him as being the one who used to sit at the Beautiful Gate of the temple to *beg* alms, and they were filled with wonder and amazement at what had happened to him" (Acts 3:9-10). These details become particularly important in our next chapter as we look more closely at Peter's understanding of how this miracle took place.

2. See John Douglas Hall, *The Cross in Our Context: Jesus and the Suffering World*, (Minneapolis: Fortress, 2003). "Luther's Theology of the Cross," Carl R. Trueman, accessed November 29, 2016, http://www.opc.org/new_horizons/NH05/10b.html; "What is cross theology / theology of the cross?" accessed November 29, 2016, http://www.gotquestions.org/cross-theology.html; "On Being a Theologian of the Cross," Gerhard Forde, accessed November 29, 2016, http://www.religion-online.org/showarticle.asp?title=320.

enemies, embodying a superior power and glory from heaven. This self-sacrificing love contrasts radically with traditional religious understandings that emphasize God as all-powerful sovereign requiring and rewarding human compliance.

In John's Gospel, we see Jesus identifying himself as the one who reveals the Father (John 1:18; 14:6-13), or is one with him (John 10:30). Jesus' glorification happens at his crucifixion (John 12:16, 23). Mark's Gospel presents the centurion as the first to confess Jesus to be the Son of God because of the way he saw him breathe his last breath (Mark 15:39). Paul emphasizes that God's otherworldly power most fully revealed in weakness on the cross in 1 Corinthians 1:18: "For the word of the cross is foolishness to those who are perishing, but to us who are being saved it is the power of God." He goes on to develop this thought in 1 Corinthians 1:21-25.

> For since in the wisdom of God the world through its wisdom did not come *to* know God, God was well-pleased through the foolishness of the message preached to save those who believe. For indeed Jews ask for signs and Greeks search for wisdom; but we preach Christ crucified, to Jews a stumbling block and to Gentiles foolishness, but to those who are the called, both Jews and Greeks, Christ the power of God and the wisdom of God. Because the foolishness of God is wiser than men, and the weakness of God is stronger than men.

In Acts 3 we see Luke's special emphasis on Jesus' death at the hands of sinners is the focal point for his proclamation of the "repentance for forgiveness of sins" to the people (Luke 24:47). Peter seizes the moment of the people's amazement to challenge what would be people's expected conclusions. Yet, Peter does not make use of the miraculous sign opportunistically to draw attention to his and John's own authority and power. Nor does he focus attention on the mechanics of how he healed the man, or on the man's faith or personal testimony. Instead of elevating the poor man now healed, clinging to him there before the crowd, Peter draws people's attention to God's elevation of the poor man par excellence—Jesus, who would otherwise be ignored and without representation there in Solomon's Portico where he once revealed himself. Moreover, Peter publically exposes the details of his audience's responsibility in the rejection and execution of Jesus, whom Israel's God glorified.

> The God of Abraham, Isaac, and Jacob, the God of our fathers, has glorified his servant Jesus, the one whom you delivered and disowned in the presence of Pilate, when he had decided to release him. But you disowned the Holy and Righteous One and asked for a murderer to be granted to you, but put to death the Prince of life, the one whom God raised from the dead, a fact to which we are witnesses. (Acts 3:13-15, emphasis mine)

Peter addresses his listeners swiftly and directly as a fellow Jew, affirming the God of Abraham, Isaac, Jacob, and "our fathers," as glorifying Jesus. Peter makes God's glorification of Jesus explicit by healing the lame man. This clarification would have been missed without his preaching. Because Peter and John were so physically engaged in the restoration of the man lame from birth, God's healing action through the name of Jesus was not visibly apparent. Acknowledgment that God glorified Jesus through this healing would also require people's acceptance of Peter's insistent word. Without Peter's interpretation of the event, onlookers would assume Peter and John were the men responsible for the miracle and worthy of the glory.

Later in Acts, in a similar story, Paul and Barnabas were hailed as gods when they healed a lame man in the pagan city of Lystra, a claim they strongly refused (Acts 14:8-18). But Peter himself, and later Paul and Barnabas, are the necessary witnesses, as God depends on his servants to bring him credit and consequent honor.

Peter's redirecting of people's attention to Jesus does not cancel out the initial emphases on his and John's loving act on behalf of the man lame from birth, which included high quality presence, advocacy, and hands-on care. The following story illustrates the value of each, their inherent dangers, and a partial response.

## REDIRECTING THE CROWD'S FOCUS TODAY

Barrio Suyapa is a neighborhood of Minas de Oro, Honduras, known for shootouts, machete fights, drunken brawls, prostitution, and abject poverty. Locals call it Barrio Olancho, after the "Wild West" department of Olancho, known for outlaws and people's justice. Gracie visited single mothers whose children came to the *Centro de Nutrition Infantil*, the village nutrition center for malnourished kids. She taught women about preventative health and helped them to plant vegetable gardens, but soon discovered that the barrio's water supply was a badly contaminated well from which women had to haul water—often hiking long distances from their mud and stick dwellings. The residents of the adjoining neighborhood, Barrio Los Calix, had organized themselves and come to us the year before, for help to establish a gravity-flow water system. After a successful installation that brought running water to hundreds of people, the adjoining neighborhood of Barrio Olancho came to us, begging us to help them too.

We worked with barrio leaders to rally the people and agreed on a plan—a major feat in a neighborhood rife with conflict. The people located a clean and accessible source of high-mountain water. The community obtained permission to put in a catch basin to pipe fresh mountain water to a distribution tank above the neighborhood. With nobody to advise us technically regarding the size of pipes needed to cover long distances up and over hills to the distribution tank and beyond to some ninety homes, we had to research and learn how to use measuring instruments to map out an effective system. We raised money from individuals and churches in the United States to buy all the pipes and cement to complete the project. The people supplied all the manual labor, and pipes from the main distribution line to their homes, faucets, sinks, and shower facilities.

The day finally came when they opened the valves of the distribution tank, and fresh water flowed from faucets and showerheads in every home. I remember the joy of witnessing the unbelief on women's faces turn to joy as they realized their days of trudging up and down the steep hillsides with water jugs atop their heads were over! Amoebic dysentery and other gastrointestinal infections soon decreased dramatically. That very day we inaugurated the project with an opening ceremony before the entire community.

We were invited to speak from atop the cement distribution tank before hundreds of neighborhood residents to celebrate the project's completion. We were truly VIPs in the barrio, and could feel people's adoration and see the potential to promote our own names, the name of our ministry Tierra Nueva, and even our own church network and country.

I was especially aware of my status as a Caucasian North American in a nation known as America's "banana republic" due to decades of United Fruit Company control. Honduras was then being pressured by the United States government to militarize, and was hosting massive joint US-Honduran military maneuvers. US military helicopters flew over Minas de Oro on a daily basis. American security interests meant Honduras would soon host the largest contingent of CIA personnel in the world. Economic aid was pouring into the country to "win hearts and minds" as the US hunkered down to direct its regional wars from what was being described as a geographic aircraft carrier. In the town, Americans had been present as representatives of gold mining companies, Catholic priests, evangelical missionaries, US Peace Corps volunteers, and even a fugitive who had gone AWOL from the US military.

I remember recognizing that it was critical in my speech to resist the adulation and point away from myself. After all, we were committed to combating the dependency mindset through promoting local self help efforts leading to empowerment— goals that now seem at odds with Peter and John's call to bring people into radical dependency on Jesus.

I chose to read John 4:4-14 and speak briefly on Jesus' encounter with the Samaritan woman at the well, where he began his relationship by asking her for a drink of water. Her question to Jesus, "How is it that you, being a Jew, ask me for a drink since I am a Samaritan woman?" and the text's note, "for Jews have no dealings with Samaritans," drew attention to the scandal of Jesus' particular race (John 4:9). Jesus erased a big religious difference between himself and Samaritans by stating "neither in this mountain nor in Jerusalem will you worship the Father." He also affirmed his own particularity, stating "salvation if from the Jews" (John 4:23). Jesus pointed the way forward for me that day. Rather than defending or debunking his own identity in a setting charged with a mixture of resentment, inferiority, prejudice, and regional pride, Jesus invited her to ask him for living water. I sought to do something similar.

That afternoon, atop the water distribution tank, I read Jesus' words in John 4:10: "If you knew the gift of God, and who it is who says to you, 'Give me a drink,' you would have asked him, and he would have given you living water." The woman responds by questioning Jesus regarding her perception that he considered himself superior to their patriarch Jacob, who gave them the well. Jesus responds by speaking truth about the limits of physical water, offering a superior spiritual water that he alone can give: "Everyone who drinks of this water will thirst again; but whoever drinks of the water that I will give him shall never thirst; but the water that I will give him will become in him a well of water springing up to eternal life" (John 4:13-14).

Though there was nothing apparently miraculous about our helping Barrio Suyapa install a gravity-flow water system, I shared how the spiritual water freely offered by the resurrected Jesus now is far superior to the cleanest mountain water that was now available to the people for cooking, washing, and watering gardens.

Over a ten-year period, we were involved in helping over twenty communities put in gravity-flow water systems. While these projects didn't include dramatic miracles (other than the generous funding of water systems), we saw the need to deflect attention away from ourselves and onto God and the people's strengths and abilities. What I did not do that day was address the people of Barrio Suyapa's common humanity with Peter and John's audience, those implicated in the rejection and killing of Jesus. I could never have imagined confronting people's tendency to deliver over, deny, and crucify Jesus as Honduras' Messiah. I wanted to offer what I thought was good news, and sought to make this news attractive, or at least positive and acceptable. Peter's message challenges me to consider how to more boldly proclaim a theology of the cross as good news to the poor.

## PRESENTING GOD'S SUFFERING SERVANT

Peter refuses any credit for the miracle, as we have already seen. But then he declares to all the people that the very God whom they worship in the temple glorifies God's servant, whom they have betrayed and killed. Peter describes Jesus as God's servant (*pais*) using special language from Isaiah, showing that he understood Jesus to embody a suffering, persecuted Messianic servant of the Lord whom God glorified.[3]

Peter's associating Jesus with the Lord's servant in Isaiah links him to the whole tradition of the redemptive suffering of this messianic figure.[4] Peter later directly states: "God announced beforehand by the mouth of all the prophets, that his Christ would suffer, he has thus fulfilled" (Acts 3:18). According to Luke's account of Jesus' appearance to the two disciples on the road to Emmaus, he himself expected his followers to understand that Scripture foretold that the Messiah would suffer. "O foolish men and slow of heart to believe in all that the prophets have spoken!"

3. This servant is presented in the Septuagint of Isaiah as the Lord's chosen one (Isa. 42:1; 49:7), whom he has placed his Spirit upon (Isa. 42:1). "I will not give my glory to another," says the Lord (Isa. 42:8), who glorifies his servant (Isa. 52:13). The term astonished (*existēmi*) appears in both Isa. 52:14 and Acts 3:10.

4. See the Septuagint of Isa. 50:6-8.

the not-yet-recognized Jesus admonishes the two disheartened disciples (Luke 24:25). "'Was it not necessary for the Christ to suffer these things and to enter into His glory?' Then beginning with Moses and with all the prophets, he explained to them the things concerning Himself in all the Scriptures" (24:26-27). Peter's evocation of Isaiah's Servant of the Lord reflects his likely understanding that Isaiah prophesied specifically about a suffering Christ who could be easily identified as finding fulfillment in Jesus, "being a man in a plague and knowing how to bear suffering . . . This one our sins he bears and he suffers for us, and we ourselves considered him to be in pain, and in a plague and in oppression" (Isa. 53:3-4).[5]

The servant's suffering was commonly understood as directly related to the distress of exile and oppression by Babylonian captors. Yet, the Greek text of Isaiah 53:8 reads, "because of the lawless deeds of *my people* he was led to death," and verse twelve reads, "he was considered with the lawless, and he took upon himself the sins of many and *because of their sins* he was delivered over" (emphasis mine).[6] Peter turns the spotlight onto his listeners, clarifying the oppressors of God's servant in Isaiah as none other than his audience—all the people gathered around him. Like a formal indictment stated before accused perpetrators, Peter presents specific and numerous charges that correspond to the conviction and crucifixion of Jesus, God's servant, described in detail in Luke's Gospel.

## PROPHETIC EXPOSURE AND THE GENERALIZATION OF BLAME

Peter speaks like an Old Testament prophet as he exposes and denounces the diverse acts that include a wide range of collaborators in the unjust killing of Jesus. Jesus is portrayed as victim

5. My translation of the Septuagint version of Isaiah, in Eugene Robert Ekblad Jr., *Isaiah's Servant Poems According to the Septuagint: An Exegetical and Theological Study*, (Leuven: Peeters, 1999), 176.

6. Ekblad, *Isaiah's Servant Poems*, 177.

of internal Jewish religious conspiracy, mob sentiment, and imperial violence in which the crowds themselves are directly implicated. Prophecy today involves exposing perpetrators and accomplices of injustice, their motives, and their methods.

The immediate backstory is Jesus' growing popularity among the masses after his proclamation of good news to the poor, healing of the blind, lame, and diseased, exorcisms of demonic powers, and embrace of the outcasts. He countered religious leaders and their legalism by demonstrating unconditional love for offenders. As he entered Jerusalem, Jesus was lauded as a conquering hero and Messiah by praising crowds. He went straight into the temple, directly challenged the corrupt system by overturning the moneychangers' tables, and confronted the hypocrisy of the religious leaders. He preached that his Kingdom was not of this world (John 18:36), and following him meant giving up worldly security and power. This made him a threat to those who benefitted from the system and didn't want to upset the Roman occupiers. They plotted to do away with him and succeeded—or so they thought.

## LOCALIZED VERSES UNIVERSAL RESPONSIBILITY FOR KILLING JESUS

In the Portico of Solomon, before the crowd astounded by the miracle, Peter includes all the people as guilty of delivering over, denying, and killing Jesus. God takes the side of the innocent victim by raising him up. This contrast between the "men of Israel's" action and God's is further specified as both Luke and Acts attribute blame for each specific crime to a wide range of perpetrators.

Judas "delivers over" (or betrays) Jesus to the chief priests and officers (Luke 22:4), who he "delivers over" to the soldiers with a kiss (Luke 22:48). The chief priests and rulers "deliver over"[7] Jesus to the Romans and to the death sentence (Luke 24:20). Peter includes in his sermon all the people who cried

7. In Mark's account, it is "the chief priests with the elders and scribes and the whole Council" who bind Jesus and deliver him to Pilate (Mark 15:1).

out (along with the chief priests and rulers) for Barabbas' release over Jesus, demanding that Pilate crucify the one called "king of the Jews" (Luke 23:13). And Pilate himself "delivers" Jesus over to the crowd's will to be crucified (Luke 23:25).

Peter describes the people as disowning or denying Jesus without directly including his own triple denial.[8] Peter repeats that the people have denied Jesus, clarifying that he is "the Holy and Righteous One"[9] prophesied by the prophet Jeremiah as the coming Messiah.[10]

Peter counts all the people guilty of injustice: "You asked for a murder to be granted to you" (Acts 3:14b). He exposes the gravity of the people's crime by revealing the divine identity of the victim: "But you put to death the Prince of Life!" (Acts 3:15a).

In other Gospel accounts, Pilate hands over Jesus to be crucified to avoid a riot (Matt. 27:20). "Wishing to satisfy the crowd" he releases Barabbas (a convicted thief), has Jesus scourged, and hands him over to be crucified (Mark 15:15). The crowd is descrribed in Matthew and Mark's account as even more active in Jesus' crucifixion than in Luke: "Those passing by were hurling abuse at Him, wagging their heads, and saying, 'Ha! you who are going *to* destroy the temple and rebuild it in three days, save yourself, and come down from the cross!'" (Matt. 27:39-40; Mark 15:29-30). The people proudly take responsibility for Jesus' death in one account, saying: "His blood shall be on us and on our children!" (Matt. 27:25).[11]

---

8. Here the verb *arneomai* is used with reference to Peter (Luke 22:57; John 13:38), an action considered a grave offense (Luke 12:9; 2 Pet. 2:1; Jude 4; 2 Tim. 2:12).

9. In the Septuagint of Isaiah 53:11, the Lord "justifies the righteous one who serves many well; and he shall bear their sins."

10. "'Behold, days are coming,' declares the Lord, 'when I will fulfill the good word which I have spoken concerning the house of Israel and the house of Judah. In those days and at that time I will cause a righteous Branch of David to spring forth; and He shall execute justice and righteousness on the earth. In those days Judah will be saved and Jerusalem will dwell in safety; and this is *the name* by which she will be called: the Lord is our righteousness'" (Jer. 33:14-16).

11. Though also included in Luke's account are a large crowd of people

## RELIGIOUS LEADERS AS PERPETRATORS

Peter clearly attributes special blame to the leaders of the people:

> Let it be known to all of you and to all the people of
> Israel, that by the name of Jesus Christ the Nazarene,
> whom you crucified, whom God raised from the
> dead—by this name this man stands here before you in
> good health. He is the stone which was rejected by you,
> the builders, but which became the chief corner stone.
> And there is salvation in no one else; for there is no
> other name under heaven that has been given among
> men by which we must be saved. (Acts 4:10-12)

The chief priests and the elders persuade the crowd (Matt.
23:20-23) and stir them up (Mark 15:11). The chief priests and
scribes mock him as he is crucified, saying, "He saved others;
he cannot save himself. Let this Christ, the King of Israel, now
come down from the cross, so that we may see and believe!"
(Mark 15:31b-32a).

In Acts, all the people are blamed for Jesus' betrayal, arrest, condemnation, and execution. They are held accountable
for what their leaders do, while the leaders are separated out for
special blame. In Peter's first sermon on the day of Pentecost, he
declares to all gathered regarding Jesus:

> Men of Israel, listen to these words: Jesus the Naza-
> rene, a man attested to you by God with miracles and
> wonders and signs which God performed through him
> in our midst, just as you yourselves know, this man,
> delivered over by the predetermined plan and fore-
> knowledge of God, you nailed to a cross by the hands
> of godless men and put him to death. (Acts 2:22-24)

He boldly identifies Jesus as Christ and God, and the
people's guilt for killing him: "Therefore let all the house of Israel know for certain that God has made him both Lord and
Christ—this Jesus whom you crucified" (Acts 2:36). But how

---

and women who followed Jesus as he made his way to be crucified, "mourn-
ing and lamenting him" (Luke 23:27).

can Jews and Gentiles living more than two thousand years later today be guilty for Jesus' rejection and death?

## UNIVERSAL ATTRIBUTION OF GUILT
## FOR REJECTING JESUS

Elsewhere in Scripture, human beings as a whole are presented as not recognizing God's revelation in Jesus. In John 1, the Word who is God, the life, and the light of all humanity, is *not recognized* by the world, and *not received* by Jesus' own people (John 1:10). Though God loves the world to such an extent that he gave his only begotten son, "men loved the darkness rather than the light, for their deeds were evil" (John 3:10). According to the Apostle Paul, both Jews and Greeks are under sin. "There is none righteous, not even one; there is none who understands, there is none who seeks for God," writes Paul. "All have turned aside, together they have become useless, there is none who does good, there is not even one."[12]

Throughout the Gospels and Acts, Psalm 118:22 is quoted as being fulfilled by the Jewish rulers, elders, and scribes' rejection of Jesus.[13] Peter crafts the Psalm into his speech to the Jewish Council regarding Jesus: "He is the stone which was rejected by you, the builders, but which became the chief corner stone" (Acts 4:11).

After the Jewish leaders prohibit Peter and John from speaking to the people in Jesus' name, Peter quotes Psalm 2 as being fulfilled. This Psalm, which speaks clearly about the non-Jewish nations' rejection of God's Messiah, is applied to include the Jewish rulers with the Gentiles' rejection of Jesus:

> Why did the Gentiles rage, and the peoples devise futile things? The kings of the earth took their stand and the rulers were gathered together against the Lord and against his Christ. For truly in this city there

12. Rom. 3:10-12 (13-18).
13. Matt. 21:42; Rom. 9:32-33; 1 Pet. 2:7.

were gathered together against your holy servant Je-
sus, whom you anointed, both Herod and Pontius
Pilate, *along with the Gentiles and the peoples of Israel.*
(Acts 4:25-27, emphasis mine)

In Matthew's Gospel, Jesus himself tells of his impending
death, including both Gentiles and Jews in the lineup of perpetrators. "Behold, we are going up to Jerusalem; and the Son of
Man will be delivered to the chief priests and scribes, and they
will condemn him to death, and will hand him over to the Gentiles to mock and scourge and crucify him, and on the third day
he will be raised up" (Matt. 20:18).

## THE OFFENSE OF JESUS THEN AND NOW

Acts presents Jesus' twelve disciples as symbolically representing
Israel's twelve tribes, the remnant who embrace Jesus as Christ. In
Acts 1:21-26, Peter presides over the replacement of Judas by Matthias so that there are twelve first-hand witnesses of Jesus' earthly
ministry and resurrection. Once the twelfth apostle is in place, the
Spirit is poured out at Pentecost. The apostles are consequently
equipped with the Holy Spirit to step into Israel's vocation to be
a blessing to all the nations. The early church begins as a Jewish
movement, and Acts documents the inclusion of the Gentiles
through their acceptance of Jesus as Israel and the world's Messiah.

Yet today there continues to be widespread resistance by
Jews and non-Jews alike to Jesus' own claims of being the only way
to the Father (John 14:6). Peter's insistence "that there is salvation
in no one else; for there is no other name under heaven that has
been given among men by which we must be saved" is rejected as
narrow, exclusive bigotry (Acts 4:12).

While visiting Israel in March 2014, I became aware of the
Hebrew acronym used by many Jews, "*Yeshu*," meaning, "may
his name be erased," revealing widespread disdain. Muslims reject Jesus' claims to be God (or any title such as "Son of God" or
"the One who reveals the Father") as blasphemous. At an out-
door worship service in a Paris park in 2014, I was preaching on

how Jesus was rejected in his day. I said this should alert us to expect similar treatment today (John 15:20). Suddenly a group of young men burned a New Testament, tried to disconnect our sound system, and threw water on us.

In mainstream Europe and North America, I run into many who express outright scorn for Jesus and his followers. They identify Christians with right wing political agendas, including opposition to gay marriage, women's rights, and the welcoming of refugees from Muslim nations.

Christians, too, can be counted amongst those who reject Jesus, when we refuse to embody, emulate, and teach God's radical way of combating evil through redemptive suffering and enemy-love. In our world of increasing terrorist attacks and violence, we need to take seriously Jesus' death on the cross as the only way to effectively overcome evil. Jesus commanded his followers:

> But I say to you who hear, love your enemies, do good to those who hate you, bless those who curse you, pray for those who mistreat you. Whoever hits you on the cheek, offer him the other also … But love your enemies, and do good, and lend, expecting nothing in return; and your reward will be great, and you will be sons of the Most High; for he himself is kind to ungrateful and evil men. Be merciful, just as your Father is merciful. (Luke 6:26-29, 35-36)

Heeding Jesus' call to love enemies and pray for persecutors is too often viewed as unrealistic. If Jesus' way of self-giving love were to spread and become a movement, there would most certainly be resistance now as there was in the first century. Jesus' own description of what it looks like to be among his followers challenges our desire for security and comfort. And yet, Jesus' teaching can strike violent offenders as strangely compelling.

## READING LUKE 6 WITH VIOLENT OFFENDERS

One night in the jail my colleague, Mike, brought his guitar and I offered to pray for the men while he sang a worship song over them. Mike sang with great tenderness as I made my way around the circle behind the men, gently placing a hand on each one's shoulder. As I prayed, I sensed a deep and mysterious outpouring of divine love for the men. By the time I made my way around the circle, many of the men were wiping tears from their eyes. I sat down and expressed how I was sensing God's huge heart for each of them.

"Can I say something?" asked a huge guy I didn't remember ever meeting.

"Yeah go for it," I said.

Humbly, he recounted a violent crime he had committed, and confessed that he even had beaten people up for pay. This led one of the gang leaders to share how he and many of the others had lots of people they hadn't forgiven whom they probably should forgive. The kindness of God seemed to be inciting a wave of repentance, which fed right into a few verses from Luke that hit home for me and the men in a fresh way. I asked someone to read Jesus' words in Luke 6:26-36.

As a well-known local criminal read Jesus' words, it felt like they were highlighted and struck home with particular authority: "But I say to you who hear, love your enemies, do good to those who hate you, bless those who curse you, pray for those who mistreat you ... Treat others the same way you want them to treat you" (Luke 6:27-28, 31).

The men were nodding at these challenging words, each nod looking like heart doors opening wider as the light of Christ flowed in like liquid medicine. Choosing to forgive and love each other was a better alternative to fights and the seclusion of lockdown—but Jesus' teaching offered more.

"If you love those who love you, what credit is that to you? For even sinners love those who love them. If you do good to those who do good to you, what credit is that to you? For even sinners do the same," the pod's shot-caller continued to a fully attentive audience (Luke 6:32-33). The codes of the street and of America's legal system were being directly challenged.

I explain that "credit" is the word *charis*, meaning grace, gift, or benefit. "As we move in the opposite spirit of enemy hate—choosing to instead love, bless, do good to and forgive—we will receive real benefits from God. And this is something we can do right here, as long as there are still enemies to love and forgive," I continue, before the final verse is read.

"But love your enemies, and do good, and lend, expecting nothing in return; and your reward will be great, and you will be sons of the Most High"—an appealing prospect to people being punished, who themselves are desperate for acceptance into a new family and the Father's embrace, regardless of their attitude (Luke 6:35a).

The final words, "for he himself is kind to ungrateful and evil men," hit us all like a big, warm, unconditional hug for thugs, inviting Jesus' call to an unheard of but strangely appealing warfare: "Be merciful, just as your Father is merciful" (Luke 6:35b-36).

In the remaining five minutes or so before the guards come, we lead the men in prayer, confessing our sins, receiving our forgiveness, forgiving ourselves, forgiving our enemies. I leave them with homework to continue the process, and it seems like we all leave having already tasted the grace, the reward for living as sons of the merciful Father—and abundant ongoing provision is available for the receiving.

## THE OFFENSE OF JESUS' MEANS OF CONFRONTING EVIL

Jesus disappointed many Jews oppressed under Roman occupation who were awaiting a jihadist-style liberator who would crush their oppressors and re-establish Israel. This expectation was even present amongst his disciples when they questioned him after his resurrection: "Lord, is it at this time you are restoring the kingdom to Israel?" (Acts 1:6). His teaching and witness are deeply challenging, inciting rejection then and now. Jesus' notion of favor run thoroughly counter to normal human aspirations for power and security in this life.

"Blessed are you who are poor, for yours is the kingdom of God," states Jesus, offering the kingdom of heaven now as people remain in poverty rather than promises of riches (Luke 6:20b). "Blessed are you who hunger now, for you shall be satisfied" affirms Jesus, promising a future satisfaction that is not guaranteed for this lifetime (Luke 6:21a). "Blessed are you who weep now," states Jesus with faith-filled confidence, promising comfort in the future (Luke 6:21b). As Israel's Messiah and the world's Savior, Jesus makes no promises to his followers about acceptance, favor in the eyes of the world, or anything akin to the "American Dream" aspiration of "life, liberty, and the pursuit of happiness."

In contrast, Jesus affirms: "Blessed are you when men hate you, and ostracize you, and insult you, and scorn your name as evil, for the sake of the Son of Man. Be glad in that day and leap for joy, for behold, your reward is great in heaven. For in the same way their fathers used to treat the prophets" (Luke 6:22-23). In contrast, Jesus strongly warns the successful: "But woe to you who are rich, for you are receiving your comfort in full. Woe to you who are well-fed now, for you shall be hungry. Woe to you who laugh now, for you shall mourn and weep. Woe to you when all men speak well of you, for their fathers used to treat the false prophets in the same way" (Luke 6:24-26).

The rise of jihadist violence throughout the world is testing the resolve of Christians to follow Jesus as God's anointed one. Beheadings, reports of violence against Kurds, Christians, and even fellow Muslims with differing views, is appalling and requires response. Retired US Marine Corps General John R. Allen's recent call to arms must be recognized as incompatible with Jesus' way:

> The execution of James Foley is an act we should not forgive nor should we forget. It embodies and brings home to us all what this group represents. The Islamic

State is an entity beyond the pale of humanity and it must be eradicated. If we delay now we will pay later.[14]

Many who value tolerance and peacemaking, Christians included, are at a loss because non-violent approaches appear impotent before those imposing a fundamentalist theocracy in the Middle East and Africa, and their military opponents led by the United States.

The United States' strategy to build a broad alliance to destroy the Islamic State enjoys broad support—especially since drones and bombing campaigns, rather than ground troops, are killing with reputed accuracy.

Yet these airstrikes are taking the lives of growing numbers of ordinary people, including many young men and women combatants from many countries drawn to jihadist activism in the prime of their lives—each one a beloved child of the God. This growing "human sacrifice" is empowering an escalation of hatred that will lead to far more death and destruction in the Middle East, Europe, and beyond. What might those who follow Jesus offer as an alternative to war on all sides?

## FOLLOWING THE CRUCIFIED MESSIAH NOW THROUGH MILITANT "VIOLENT" NONVIOLENCE

In the place of Christian passivism or other common forms of non-violent resistance, I suggest that Jesus followers recognize and embrace his specific approach to resisting evil. I somewhat reluctantly will refer to Jesus' approach as "militant 'violent' non-violence."[15] On one hand, Jesus refused to use violence against human beings no matter how antagonistic. He modeled non-violence or even anti-violence towards people. On the other

---

14. "Destroy the Islamic State Now," Gen. John Allen, last modified August 20, 2014, accessed December 1, 2016, http://www.defenseone.com/ideas/2014/08/gen-allen-destroy-islamic-state-now/92012/.

15. Non-violent resistance is often associated with passivism, which sounds disengaged or "passive."

hand, Jesus practiced a kind of prophetic and deeply spiritual violence that must be rediscovered today if God's reign on earth is to make a visible difference.

Jesus begins his ministry after his baptism, departure into the wilderness, and re-entry as the new kind of Joshua. Jesus enacted God's saving action through consistently distinguishing human beings from invisible predatory powers. Jesus loved people through healing, freeing, cleansing, recruiting, teaching, challenging, rebuking, forgiving, commissioning, and other contextually appropriate actions.

At the same time, Jesus identified and mercilessly attacked the invisible predatory powers that occupied human beings and institutions he encountered: evil spirits, sickness, legalism, superiority, discrimination, religious spirits, death, and other forces (Eph. 6:12). He cast out demons, confronted arrogant law-enforcers, exposed hypocrisy, rebuked wind and waves, drove out money changers from the temple, broke down the dividing wall, and abolished the enmity and the law of commandments contained in ordinances and put hatred to death (Eph 2:14-16). What might this look like today?

Jesus invades territory occupied by the ruler of this world (John 12:31), destroying his works (1 John 3:8). Jesus' first miracle in the Gospels of Mark and Luke is to cast out unclean spirits from a man in the synagogue—most certainly a confrontational act followed by many acts of liberation.[16] What might it look like to recover this "not of this world" militancy today?

In the Gospel accounts, you will find no place where Jesus himself kills or harms anyone, including his Jewish enemies and the Roman occupiers of Palestine. Jesus never calls on others to exercise violence against human beings or legitimates appropriate defense of the homeland. Not even once!

When his cousin, John the Baptist, is beheaded by Herod, rather than calling for vengeance, Jesus withdraws to a secluded place where he is moved by compassion for a crowd of 5,000 who pursues him, whom he heals, teaches, and then feeds (Matt.

16. Matt. 8:16; 9:32-33; Mark 1:34; 5:1-20.

14:13ff). Jesus commanded his followers to love and forgive their enemies, and to pray for persecutors. Jesus taught his followers to flee to the mountains when they see Jerusalem surrounded by armies rather than sacrifice their life in homeland defense.[17]

Jesus' practice must be discerned and embraced as the standard for now, and Christians must renounce the use of physical violence as "the legitimate use of force," replacing it with radical love of enemies, prophetic exposure of injustice, Spirit-guided and empowered acts promoting reconciliation and peace, intercession, prayer and fasting, acts of service and mercy, all life-giving acts embodying Paul's admonition "do not be overcome by evil, but overcome evil with good" (Rom. 12:21), and more.

Jesus in his earthly mission was "militant," combative, and aggressive in his confrontations with evil as he proclaimed the good news of the Kingdom of God. Jesus' activism and unique "violence" must challenge the fearful and passive attitudes of many who resist proactive engagement with people caught up in violence against humans and creation.

In February 2015, we saw the Jesus-like witness of twenty-one Coptic Christians who cried out in unison just before being beheaded by ISIS in Libya "*Ya Rabbi Yasou*" (O My Lord Jesus). We live in a time of growing rejection of Jesus and persecution of his followers throughout the world. Now it is important that we who call ourselves Christian attune our lives to Jesus' teaching and person like never before. What could it look like to live our lives more fully "in the name of Jesus?"

---

17. See Bob Ekblad, *A New Christian Manifesto: Pledging Allegiance to the Kingdom of God*, (Louisville: Westminster John Knox, 2008), 146-148.

# 6

# Transformation in Whose Name?

eter and John are naturally in the spotlight as the newly
healed and empowered man clings to them and the
crowd runs to them. These men of God visibly empowered by the Spirit could have leveraged their success to maxi-
mize influence. The temptation to take credit for the lame man's
healing and garner adherents to themselves as leaders of the
new Jesus movement must have been strong. This continues to
be a very real temptation for disciples today. These are inherent
dangers of ministries that highlight strong relational presence,
hands-on action, healing, or any significant physical benefit or
attention being drawn to human change agents or their beneficiaries rather than to Jesus.

As we saw in the previous chapter, Peter takes the spotlight
off himself and John, refocusing the crowd's attention on their
own guilt for having delivered over, denied, and killed Jesus. After such visible success they may have been tempted to downplay
prophetic critique in order to minimize offense to stay in a positive flow. But instead Peter goes on to affirm that the strengthen-
ing of the man's feet and ankles was not accomplished by them,
but through the name of this crucified Jesus whom God consequently glorified and will continue to elevate.

Peter demonstrates something critical for ministry activists
today. The only way people could know the true subject of the
hidden work of Jesus is for believers to publically give him the
credit. This keeps them from looking like the saviors, making

room for Jesus to be announced as Israel's awaited Messiah, now resurrected and ascended.

Paul writes, "If you confess with your mouth Jesus as Lord, and believe in your heart that God raised him from the dead, you will be saved" (Rom. 10:9). Paul quotes the same passage from Joel 2:32 that Peter cites in his sermon, insisting that the "Lord is Lord of all, abounding in riches for all who call on Him—for 'whoever will call on the name of the Lord will be saved'" (Rom. 10:12-13). In order for people to believe in Jesus and call on him, someone must announce Jesus, which is exactly what Peter is modeling here.

"How then will they call on Him in whom they have not believed? How will they believe in him whom they have not heard? And how will they hear without a preacher? How will they preach unless they are sent? Just as it is written, 'How beautiful [*hōraios* as in "*beautiful gate*"] are the feet of those who bring good news of good things!'" (Rom. 10:14-15).

## HEALING IN JESUS' NAME IN AN ASIAN SLUM

During a twenty-four-hour stopover in an unnamed Asian megacity in 2012, I had the opportunity to visit a slum community of squatters that had been ravaged by fires and forced evictions. Two young women, doing ministry work among the poorest of the poor, had gained the trust of the residents through humbly living among the people for several years. They played with the children and advocated for the whole community. Then, mafia-like land developers assailed the neighborhood with a scheme. The developers claimed that people's houses would be imminently bulldozed by the landowners, who were reclaiming their land from the slum community. However, if people accepted a minimal payment before that happened, they would at least receive some benefit. Otherwise, they risked receiving nothing. While in the beginning there was vocal and organized resistance, families left their homes by night in increasing numbers after caving in to the pressure and receiving payment.

I walked with Susan (not her real name) through the bull-dozed ruins, listening to the heartbreaking story. Muslim prayer towers (minarets) loomed on both sides, calling adherents to prayer through loud speakers throughout the day. We stopped and spoke with one of the residents, an impoverished woman who was holding out for a higher offer from the developers before abandoning her home.

After listening to this woman share about how difficult it was for her to leave her home of more than fifteen years, I asked Susan if she could ask whether the woman was suffering from back pain, based on what I thought might be a prophetic impression. The woman said that she in fact did suffer from chronic and crippling back pain. I asked her, through Susan, if we could lay hands on her and pray for her to be healed, and she said she yes, she did want prayer. I explained that we would be praying in Jesus' name and asked her if this was okay, and she agreed. Standing there in the rubble-strewn roadway in front of her slum dwelling, with our eyes open, Susan put a hand on the woman's back and we spoke out loud, ordering the pain to go out in Jesus' name.

The woman expressed her gratitude and we said our good-byes, not thinking to ask her if she felt any improvement. We moved on to talk to people in the adjoining houses. Having experienced immediate healing, the woman told her surrounding neighbors. There, at the next house, women came to us, one after another, requesting prayer for various ailments. We prayed for abscessed teeth, pain throughout the body and back, and shoulder pain. We asked each person their permission to pray in Jesus' name. People agreed, and were healed as we prayed. Joy and excitement were visible on people's faces. One woman pulled her husband over and insisted that we pray for his heart murmurs and pain. As we prayed, we proclaimed Jesus' victory over the powers of pain and disease, and people received our ministry without resistance.

A young Indonesian lawyer who represented the slum dwellers was watching while people were getting healed. He approached me and asked whether I prayed for land. He asked if we could pray for a legal breakthrough for the poor families he represented, who had not yet received remuneration for their homes. A whole circle of people gathered around as we explained to the lawyer how we would pray if he wanted us to do so.

"We understand that God is our father and your father, and the earth and everything in it belongs to him," I explained, with Susan interpreting. "The enemy of God, Satan, is ruling the world. But we believe that God sent his son, Jesus, to destroy the power of the Enemy, by dying on the cross. God has raised Jesus from the dead, and he is now at the right hand of the Father. He intercedes for us, and sends the Holy Spirit to be our advocate and defender. Is it okay with you if we pray for Jesus to intercede for you, and to send the Holy Spirit to help you with these problems?" The lawyer and all the people expressed their agreement, and we prayed. I was amazed to see people's total openness to prayer in Jesus' name.

On our way back, we passed by a woman in the doorway of her house (another *beautiful gate*), and the thought, "Pain in her left hip," dropped into my mind. Ignoring this, I continued walking with my hostess. After telling her about this impression, she said that we should definitely go back and ask the woman. We did, and, sure enough, she was in pain and wanted prayer for her hip and her knees. We asked if we could pray for her "in Jesus' name," and she agreed without hesitation. She was healed immediately, and moved that God had revealed her hip problem. Another neighbor who washed clothes by hand for a living asked us to pray for her elbow. She, too, was healed on the spot. Susan had not previously witnessed physical healing. She was watching in amazement as her neighbors received immediate healing in the midst of hands-on prayer. Like Peter and John, the two of us were witnesses to God's healing power mediated through our presence and actions. That these actions were done "in the name of Jesus" in and among Muslims between two towering minarets drew attention to Jesus' special agency as their unconditional healer.

In this moment, Susan and I did not spend adequate time teaching those who were healed about Jesus, or inviting them to give their lives to him. Nor did I anticipate the repercussions for Susan, who was attacked by crippling and prolonged pain, which began the night after praying for and witnessing all this healing. Persecution in the aftermath of the in-breaking of Jesus' Kingdom can include spiritual attacks that must be anticipated and prepared for. These experiences have shown me how ministry of presence and prayer must include proclamation, discipleship, and spiritual warfare as integral parts of holistic ministry.

## FAITH IN THE NAME OF JESUS OF NAZARETH

Insistence that healing happens in the name of the actual Jesus born in Nazareth, executed by the authorities, confessed to be alive, and ascended to the Father, appears to be considered essential by the writer of Acts. Earlier in Luke, details are provided about Jesus' hometown, showing Jesus' pedigree, links to Israel's Davidic line, in fulfillment of ancient prophesies of a coming Messiah. These important details ground the early church confession that this particular man, Jesus of Nazareth, is the cosmic Christ.

Luke's Gospel specifies Jesus' hometown of Nazareth numerous times to situate him as a particular historic, geographically grounded figure who fulfills Israel's anticipated coming Messiah in precise ways. Nazareth is where the angel, Gabriel, announced the miraculous birth of Jesus to Mary, whom he presented as God's Son and Israel's Messiah, descended from David (Luke 1:26). "He will be great and will be called the Son of the Most High; and the Lord God will give him the throne of his father David; and he will reign over the house of Jacob forever, and his kingdom will have no end" (Luke 2:32-33). In his words to Mary in Nazareth, Gabriel makes direct reference to Jesus as fulfilling Nathan's prophesy in 2 Samuel 7:12-16.

Joseph leaves Nazareth with his pregnant wife, Mary, for his birthplace, Bethlehem. Luke emphasizes that this was to comply with Caesar Augusts' first census, done "while Quirinius was governor of Syria," and that Joseph was "of the house and family of David" (Luke 2:1-4).

Later, Joseph and Mary move to Nazareth in Galilee after presenting Jesus in the temple, when he was eight days old (Luke 2:21, 39). After his baptism and temptation in the desert, Jesus is described as going to Nazareth "where he was brought up" (Luke 4:16). Luke recounts that Jesus read from the scroll of the prophet Isaiah and preached a prophetic message that resulted in his compatriots driving him out of his hometown (Luke 4:28-30). Peter proclaims that it is precisely faith in the name of *this* Jesus, whom the people have killed and whom God has raised from the dead, that heals the lame man.

## UPON THE FAITH IN JESUS' NAME

However, when Peter preaches about Jesus before the gathered crowd in the Portico of Solomon, he begins by referring to the most recent events about Jesus and doesn't mention his city of origin, Nazareth. Peter proclaims that the dramatic healing was done in the name of the Jesus the people had recently delivered over, denied, and killed, whom God raised from the dead. He does this not by presenting the name as a magic incantation that must contain exact words in order to be effective, but with precise minimalist language that I offer in my own word-for-word translation of Acts 3:16 here: "And upon the faith in [or "from"] his name—the name has strengthened this one [man] whom you see and know; and the faith through him has given him this perfect health in the presence of you all."[1]

---

1. This unique expression in Greek (καὶ ἐπὶ τῇ πίστει τοῦ ὀνόματος αὐτοῦ τοῦτον ὃν θεωρεῖτε καὶ οἴδατε, ἐστερέωσεν τὸ ὄνομα αὐτοῦ, καὶ ἡ πίστις ἡ δι᾽ αὐτοῦ ἔδωκεν αὐτῷ τὴν ὁλοκληρίαν ταύτην ἀπέναντι πάντων ὑμῶν) is often inadequately translated in ways that could reinforce an instrumentalist reading of this verse. The NASV says, "and on the basis of faith in His name, it is the name of Jesus which has strengthened this man"—an accurate translation. The ESV renders: "And his name—by faith in his name—has made this man strong whom you see and know, and the faith that is through Jesus has given the man this perfect health in the presence of you all."

This word-for-word translation of the Greek of Peter's words is awkward but potentially helpful in its precision. The Greek word underlying the English "upon" is *epi*.[2] It is upon the faith "in" (or, more literally, "from") his name that *beautiful gate* activity happens. Peter's words appear to mean that it is "upon" the faith *that comes from* the invisible Jesus that events take place, which include healing and empowerment to cross through the *beautiful gate*. This idea is further clarified by the second half of Acts 3:16, which reads, "and the faith *through him* has given him this perfect health in the presence of you all" (emphasis mine). Faith is a gift from God, as Paul writes to the Ephesians. "For by grace you have been saved through faith; and that not of your-selves, *it is* the gift of God; not as a result of works, so that no one may boast" (Eph. 2:8-9). This faith "from the name" includes Peter and John, the man lame from birth, and Jesus himself.

After the rulers, elders, and scribes arrest Peter and John, and throw them in prison, they prohibit them from speaking or teaching anyone "upon this name"[3] or "upon the name of Jesus."[4]

But what does "upon the faith" in Jesus' name, or "the faith through him," actually mean? Faith in Jesus' name means faith in the invisible Jesus no longer physically present and visible as he was during his earthly life. Living "by faith" is acting in "the assurance of *things* hoped for, the conviction of things *not seen*" (Heb. 11:1, emphasis mine). Jesus himself modeled this faith re-garding his invisible Father, and people did not receive him or believe: "I have come in my Father's name, and you do not receive me" (John 5:43). To those who had questioned whether he was the Christ when he walked in the Portico of Solomon, he stated: "I told you, and you do not believe; the works that I do *in my Father's name*, these testify of me" (John 10:25, emphasis mine).

2. The use of ἐπὶ with the dative can mean "on" or "upon," referring to "that upon which a state of being, an action, or a result is based" (William Bauer, *A Greek-English Lexicon of the New Testament and other Early* Christian *Literature*, trans. William F. Arndt and F. Wilbur Gingrich [Chicago: University of Chicago, 1979], 287).

3. Acts 4:17, ἐπὶ τῷ ὀνόματι τούτῳ.

4. Acts 4:18, ἐπὶ τῷ ὀνόματι τοῦ Ἰησοῦ.

Peter models confidence in the ascended Christ, enabling him to heal in Jesus' name, inspiring us to do likewise. Many people are timid about exercising such authority, which seems presumptuous. A widespread way of praying is to say: "God, if it is your will, please heal…" Asking God to heal comes from a way of understanding Jesus' instruction to his disciples regarding prayers of petition. "Truly, truly, I say to you, if you ask the Father for anything in my name, he will give it to you" (John 16:23, 26-27). Prayers of petition or intercession to God are important but different than direct commands in Jesus' name. Peter acts in alignment with Jesus' practice and teaching regarding direct commands for healing,[5] deliverance,[6] and dealing with natural phenomenon like storms.[7] The seventy are sent out on a mission to themselves "heal the sick" (Luke 10:9). They return with joy: "Lord, even the demons are subject to us in your name" (Luke 10:17).

Peter evades all credit for this faith as a human work by emphasizing Jesus' name and Jesus himself as the source of this faith: "It is the faith that comes through him that has given this complete healing to him, as you can all see" (Acts 3:16). Receiving this faith that comes from Jesus is accessed through a posture of spiritual openness, active listening, and receiving, which happens when we pray. This posture is different from trying to make things happen through invoking Jesus' name from out of a rational belief system, positive attitude, or desperate need.

## THE SONS OF SCEVA'S FORMULAIC USE OF JESUS' NAME IN ACTS 19

I lead a Bible study on the name of Jesus with prison inmates in Washington State Reformatory. We contemplate together the reasons why the sons of Sceva failed to drive out demons in Jesus' name in Acts 19. This story presents a powerful critique of the

5. Matt. 10:8; Luke 4:39.
6. Mark 9:25; Luke 4:35, 41; 9:42.
7. Mark 4:39; Luke 8:24.

misuse of Jesus' name as a technique to fix a problem. After brief introductions and an opening prayer, I invite someone to read Acts 19:11-12: "God was performing extraordinary miracles by the hands of Paul, so that handkerchiefs or aprons were even carried from his body to the sick, and the diseases left them and the evil spirits went out."

A number of men serving life sentences are among us, one of whom is deeply spiritual. His name is Rogelio, and he participates in many of the Christian services offered by volunteers, reads and studies his Bible, and recruits others to participate in our bi-weekly Spanish service. I look at him and ask the men what people would think if handkerchiefs, tissues, or maybe prison-issue T-shirts that Rogelio prayed over were passed around to people, leading to miraculous healings and deliverance from evil spirits in the prison.

The men laugh and Rogelio blushes. Everyone agrees that if miracles like this broke out, it would cause a big stir and would definitely boost Rogelio's standing as a man of God. They could see the potential for abuse, as anointed objects could easily be incorporated into the prison system's underground currency. People with the special powers could do favors for people and then want their "get back." People on the margins are all familiar with schemes by charlatan healers to sell blessed water or oil. Theirs is a world where witchcraft is common, including paying *curanderos* (witches) to curse enemies or to break curses over themselves, burning candles to the *Santa Muerte* (Saint of Death), buying lottery tickets, or gambling in casinos with superstitious faith.

Most of the men come from Mexican or Central American backgrounds and grew up Catholic. They are familiar with traditional magical understandings of holy water, the power of saying Hail Marys, and crossing themselves religiously, often in very particular ways. Many were familiar with the magical understanding of the liturgy and Eucharist common among the people participating in the traditional Roman Catholic Mass. New inmates often attend Bible studies with me expecting that "doing their religious time" will improve their luck. It was easy for everyone to see how Jewish exorcists in the following verses would seek to practice Paul's ministry like a method. I invite a volunteer to read Acts 19:13-14, and ask them to look more closely at the details of the story. A younger man only six months into his first ever prison sentence volunteers to read:

> But also some of the Jewish exorcists, who went from place to place, attempted to name over those who had the evil spirits the name of the Lord Jesus, saying, "I adjure you by Jesus whom Paul preaches." Seven sons of one Sceva, a Jewish chief priest, were doing this. (Acts 19:13-14)

I ask the men what exactly the Jewish exorcists were doing, and the men looked at their Bibles. People note that the exorcists were each trying to exercise the same authority and power that Paul exercised by using the name Paul used. They were speaking the name "Lord Jesus" over people who had demons. We notice how each give orders, "I order you by Jesus," and how they add the name "Paul" in an attempt to increase their credibility before the demons.

"Let's see how that worked for them," I suggest, asking someone to read Acts 19:15-16. The same man reads again, eager to gain credibility as the newest member of the group of veteran prisoners.

> And the evil spirit answered and said to them, "I recognize Jesus, and I know about Paul, but who are you?" And the man, in whom was the evil spirit, leaped on them and subdued all of them and overpowered them, so that they fled out of that house naked and wounded.

"So what happened to these sons of Sceva guys when they try to use Jesus' name?" I ask the men.

"The evil spirits recognize Jesus, they only know about Paul," someone says. "But they don't see the others as having any authority and take them out," another guy adds.

I search for a relevant example. "Maybe it would be like if I didn't really know Rogelio personally, but I'd heard of him and had some kind of connection, and then went to some gangster *mafioso* drug lords who know him, and dropped his name to get a favor. Then, to check me out, to be sure I was legit, they ask me some questions about Rogelio and can see that I really don't know him at all. That might put me in a dangerous place, don't you think?" I ask.

Rogelio nods his agreement and launches into a story about how he actually sent someone to do a favor for him with some high-level Mexican drug cartel people.

"These guys didn't trust my friend and took him outside and walked him around their property like they were going to do him in or something," recounted Rogelio. "And these guys don't have any qualms about killing someone. One of them had killed over twenty people. They didn't do anything to him, but it totally freaked out my friend."

"And that's kind of what happened to the people who heard about how the sons of Sceva got beaten up," I suggest. "Can someone read Acts 19:17?" I ask.

> This became known to all, both Jews and Greeks, who lived in Ephesus; and fear fell upon them all and the name of the Lord Jesus was being magnified.

"So what does this tell you about the name of the Jesus?" I ask them after the verse was read.

"You can't just use Jesus' name to do whatever you want," Rogelio says. "You have to be in the flow of what God is up to and not just be about your own thing."

"Jesus' name is powerful when it is invoked by people who know him," I say. "Let's check out some other verses that I think are related to this," I continue, inviting people to turn to and read Matthew 7:21-23:

> Not everyone who says to me, "Lord, Lord," will enter the kingdom of heaven, but he who does the will of my Father who is in heaven will enter. Many will say

to me on that day, "Lord, Lord, did we not prophesy in your name, and in your name cast out demons, and in your name perform many miracles?" And then I will declare to them, "I never knew you; depart from me, you who practice lawlessness."

Reading this scripture really impacts the men. They can see that the sons of Sceva were operating as lone rangers, which backfired. Jesus calls this lawlessness—doing what's right in your own eyes rather than being in alignment with the will of God. Even if you're doing important spiritual-looking work. These may be counterfeit miracles, prophesy, and the like, which can be practiced without knowing Jesus.

I invite someone to read Philippians 3:7-11, where Paul recounts how his good Jewish bloodline and all the good things he was about as a religious zealot were nothing but rubbish compared with coming to know Jesus in a personal way.

But whatever things were gain to me, those things I have counted as loss for the sake of Christ. More than that, I count all things to be loss in view of the surpassing value of knowing Christ Jesus my Lord, for whom I have suffered the loss of all things, and count them but rubbish so that I may gain Christ, and may be found in him, not having a righteousness of my own derived from the law, but that which is through faith in Christ, the righteousness which comes from God on the basis of faith, that I may know him and the power of his resurrection and the fellowship of his suffering, being conformed to his death, in order that I may attain to the resurrection from the dead. (Phil. 3:7-11)

This scripture also made a big impact, as the prisoners could see the difference between good looking actions and a superior righteousness that comes out of being in the flow of knowing Jesus.

"So let's check out these next verses of Acts 19:19-20 and see how the rest of the story plays out," I say.

Many also of those who had believed kept coming, confessing and disclosing their practices. And many of those who practiced magic brought their books together and began burning them in the sight of everyone; and they counted up the price of them and found it fifty thousand pieces of silver. So the word of the Lord was growing mightily and prevailing.

"So, how did the people respond after freaking out about the Jewish exorcists getting beaten up by the demon-possessed guy?" I ask the men.

We had a great discussion about how people were seeing that the extraordinary miracles done by the Apostle Paul had nothing to do with magic. Rather, Paul was operating out of an active relationship with the resurrected Jesus, whom he knew personally and was working in full alignment with. This caused people to want the authentic, to the point that they were willing to confess and renounce their occult practices.

This story shows that it's not about knowing techniques or having special knowledge from books, such as the magic books people leaned on, or even the Bible. Healing or casting out evil spirits in Jesus' name happens best when we are doing it from a place of unity and total alignment with Jesus' will on the earth. We concluded our time inviting the Spirit to search our hearts to show us anything we are leaning on for authority and power other than Jesus that we should confess and turn away from. Our final prayer included a time to recommit ourselves to pursuing a relationship with Jesus by faith.

## THE THREAT AND POWER OF JESUS' NAME

Returning to Acts 3:1-4:21, we can see from our prison Bible study perspective the perils of using the name of Jesus instrumentally for power, or as a name to drop, or a currency to spend to get what you want. Faith in Jesus' name is not about engaging in an action done verbally "in Jesus' name" in a way that gets all the words just right—like keying in a pin number to withdraw money from an ATM, typing in a password to gain access to an account, or inserting the right key to open a door. Acts 3 does not support an instrumentalist or magic use of Jesus' name, which appears to be prohibited by the third commandment: "You shall not take the name of the Lord your God in vain, for the Lord will not leave him unpunished who takes his name in vain" (Exod. 20:7).

Yet, when Peter and John say, "In the name of Jesus Christ the Nazarene—walk!" and a man who has been lame for forty years is instantly healed, authorities interrogate them, wanting technical details about how this change could occur: "By what power, or in what name, have you done this?" (Acts 4:7).

Peter's explanation is remarkably simple and direct, compelling them to believe and accept his interpretation of the story.

> Rulers and elders of the people, if we are on trial today for a benefit done to a sick man, as to how this man has been made well, let it be known to all of you and to all the people of Israel, that in the name of Jesus Christ the Nazarene, whom you crucified, whom God raised from the dead—in this name this man stands here before you in good health. (Acts 4:8-10)

Peter appeals to his crossexaminers with humor and logic, expecting them to take the empirical evidence seriously of the once-lame man standing before them, now in perfect health. This reasoned appeal forms the basis for his charge that they are the builders referred to in Psalm 118:22-23 who fulfill this prophesy in their crucifixion and rejection of Jesus: "He is the stone which was rejected by you, the builders, but which became the chief corner stone" (Acts 4:11).

Peter is unapologetic that Jesus is the only savior, and his name the only name that saves. "And there is salvation in no one else; for there is no other name under heaven that has been given among men by which we must be saved" (Acts 4:12).

In the next scene, the religious leaders are said to notice Peter and John's confidence, that they'd been with Jesus, they see the man standing with them healed, and have nothing to say in response. We as readers are offered an inside look at discussions amongst the rulers, elders, and scribes, who fully acknowledge the validity of the miraculous healing.

> What shall we do with these men? For the fact that a noteworthy miracle has taken place through them is apparent to all who live in Jerusalem, and we cannot deny it. But so that it will not spread any further among the people, let us warn them to speak no longer to any man in this name. (Acts 4:16)

Regardless of the legitimacy of the healing as a sign confirming Peter and John's proclamation, we see that the religious leaders' biggest concern appears to be that "it" (faith in the name of Jesus) would spread further amongst the people who have believed the message, which we've just been told "came to be about five thousand" men after Peter's sermon (Acts 4:4). Believing in the name of Jesus threatens the dominant religious systems because of the empowering nature of life "in Jesus' name" that renders obsolete the old hierarchies. Let's now explore the fuller picture a life of faith inside Jesus' name.

## FAITH IN(SIDE) JESUS' NAME

Faith in Jesus' name shifts the believer's entire being, relationships, and realm of influence into God's presence and moves them into Jesus' Kingdom now. We saw in chapter four the inseparable synergy of the man lame from birth's seeing and asking, Peter's fixing his gaze, speaking to the man twice, his direct assistance seizing him by the right hand, and raising him up in the name of Jesus. Yet, in the way the story is told, the text actually puts far more attention on the actions of the lame man than on Peter and John.

Acts 3:1-10 highlights the man's agency from the start. His initial four actions of seeing and asking Peter and John, giving them his attention, and expecting to receive from them, are accompanied by five of Peter's actions (Peter fixes his gaze on him, asks him to look at him, speaks to him, seizes him by the right hand and raises him up). Peter's actions are followed by seven verbs of movement by the man lame from birth, in contrast to the five by Peter. The man leaps, stands upright, walks, enters the temple, walks, leaps, and praises God. All of these many actions of Peter and the man lame from birth, were indicated as done "in the name of Jesus the Nazarene."

"In the name of Jesus the Nazarene"[8] can best be understood as a spiritual state or "flow" inside God's presence or "name"[9] that includes Peter, John, the Holy Spirit upon them, the lame man, and Jesus himself.[10] When Peter and John are brought before Annas the high priest, Caiaphas, John, Alexander, and others of high priestly descent, they affirm that the once-lame man is standing now completely healed "in [or within] the name of Jesus."

> Know this you and everyone else in Israel. It is *in the name of Jesus Christ of Nazareth*, whom you crucified but whom God raised from the dead, that this man stands before you complexly healed.
> (Acts 4:10, emphasis mine)

Peter preaches and invites his hearers to fully step inside God's name revealed as Jesus the Christ. In the next chapter I will explore the role of repentance, conversion, and baptism in the Holy Spirit in crossing over this line through the *beautiful gate*.

Early church fathers in the eastern tradition of Christianity understood being in Jesus' name as a state people can enter

8. ἐν τῷ ὀνόματι Ἰησοῦ Χριστοῦ τοῦ Ναζωραίου.

9. The Hebrew equivalent to the Greek ἐν (in), as in "*in* the name," is the particle *beth*, as in *be-shem* (in the name). *Beth* includes a broad range of meetings, including "in," "with," "within," or "inside," that supports this holistic notion of all of the characters being inside or within Jesus' name.

10. "In ἐν τῷ ὀνόματι, the attitude is static; it expresses the repose which follows the attainment of the goal and a certain interiorization or immanence; our spirit is transported "into" the name, within the name, it is united to the name and makes its abode there" (A Monk of the Eastern Church [Fr. Lev Gillet], *The Jesus Prayer* [Crestwood: St. Vladimir's Seminary Press, 1987], 27).

and stay within through continuous invocation of Jesus' name through the "Jesus Prayer," also known as the "Prayer of the Heart." While the content of this prayer has evolved over time,[11] it originates in two Gospel stories that are combined: that of the publican in the temple who beats his chest and cries out, "God, be merciful to me, the sinner!" (Luke 18:13), and the blind man who cries out, "Jesus, Son of David, have mercy on me!" (Luke 18:38). What was most important for the early monastics was Jesus' victory over the powers through his emptying himself, becoming a servant to the point of death on a cross, as described in Philippians 2:10-11:

> For this reason also, God highly exalted Him, and be-
> stowed on Him the name which is above every name,
> so that at the name of Jesus every knee will bow, of
> those who are in heaven and on earth and under the
> earth, and that every tongue will confess that Jesus
> Christ is Lord, to the glory of God the Father.

These early monks in the eastern tradition drew confidently from this ancient hymn, and many other scriptures, as a basis for spiritual warfare against the forces of evil that sabotage the believer's life of faith, as in this excerpt from the Philokalia:

> A monk should constantly call: "Lord, Jesus Christ,
> Son of God, have mercy upon me!" in order that this
> remembering of the name of our Lord Jesus Christ
> should incite him to battle with the enemy. By this re-
> membrance a soul forcing itself to this practice can dis-
> cover everything which is within, both good and bad.
> First it will see within, in the heart, what is bad, and
> later- what is good. This remembrance is for rousing
> the serpent, and this remembrance is for subduing it.
> This remembrance can reveal the sin living in us, and
> this remembrance can destroy it. This remembrance
> can arouse all the enemy hosts in the heart, and little
> by little this remembrance can conquer and uproot

11. See A Monk of the Eastern Church, *The Jesus Prayer*,
and Irénée Hausherr, *The Name of Jesus*, trans. Charles Cummings
(Michigan: Cistercian Publications, 1978).

them. The name of our Lord Jesus Christ, descending into the depths of the heart, will subdue the serpent holding sway over the pastures of the heart, and will save our soul and bring it to life. Thus abide constantly with the name of our Lord Jesus Christ, so that the heart swallows the Lord and the Lord the heart, and the two become one. But this work is not done in one or two days; it needs many years and a long time. For great and prolonged labor is needed to cast out the foe so that Christ dwells in us.[12]

I first became aware of this tradition through the nineteenth century Russian spiritual classics *The Way of the Pilgrim* and *The Pilgrim Continues His Way*, wherein the anonymous narrator recounts his journey across Russia seeking understanding as to how to practice Paul's call for believers to pray without ceasing (1 Tim. 5:17). While the pilgrim himself begins by reciting the Jesus Prayer thousands of times daily in a rote, religious way, he describes the process wherein the prayer moves from the lips to the mind and then descends into the heart, becoming ceaseless invocation and communion with God. This made me long for a deeper experience of God's Spirit that was not effort-driven but natural—or supernatural.

I began invoking Jesus' name throughout the day, seeking to practice deliberately imagining Jesus' name going from a whisper on my lips into my mind through active meditation on the Jesus of the Gospels. I followed the counsels of the writers of the *Philokalia*,[13] *The Way of the Pilgrim*,[14] and other writers on the Prayer of the Heart, and began to experience the invocation of Jesus descending into my heart and rising from deep inside me to God—though it always seemed to take deliberate effort and

12. E. Kadloubovsky and G.E.H. Palmer, *The Writings from the Philokalia on the Prayer of the Heart* (London: Faber and Faber, 1992), 222-223.

13. St. Hesychios the Priest, "On Watchfulness and Holiness," in *The Philokalia: The Complete Text, Volume One*, trans. G. E. H. Palmer, Philip Sherrard, and Kallistos Ware, (London: Faber and Faber, 1979), 161-198.

14. *The Way of a Pilgrim and The Pilgrim Continues His Way*, trans. Olga Savin (Boston: Shambhala Publications, 2001).

even discipline. I still experienced benefit, finding that calling out to Jesus continually as a sinner in need of mercy helps me to survive and even succeed as a parent, as a husband, and a pastor. My spiritual thirst grew as I prayed, and I found myself longing for a deeper connection to God.

Faith in Jesus' name must be understood in this eastern Christian sense of being in a state of actively moving in the flow of Jesus' invisible presence through ceaseless prayer. In Acts 3-4, faith in the name of Jesus is a spiritual, relational space that includes Peter, John, the man lame from birth, and anyone who subsequently responds to the preaching of the word. Faith in Jesus' name was what Susan and I experienced together with her neighbors in the Asian slum community. Faith in the name of Jesus happens at the threshold of the *beautiful gate,* as well as in the before and after. Ideally, it also includes each and every part of the process of moving from outside to inside the community of the believers. Inside Jesus' name, everything is aligned, and timing is of the utmost importance because life is happening by faith in Jesus' name.

Living a life of faith in Jesus' name will inevitably lead to opposition from the invisible demonic powers, like those that assailed the sons of Sceva, and from the powers behind religious and political systems that incarcerated, interrogated, and prohibited the apostles' mission. At any rate, in the face of opposition, the apostles affirm their commitment to practicing Jesus' ministry as he practiced in the Gospels, "in Jesus name," as stated powerfully in their prayer in our final verse: "And now, Lord, take note of their threats, and grant that your bond-servants may speak your word with all confidence, while you extend your hand to heal, and signs and wonders take place through the name of your holy servant Jesus" (Acts 4:29-30).

Moving into an active spiritual life in Jesus' name means identifying, renouncing, and moving away from dependency on other names and securities, and turning more fully towards Jesus, which we will now explore.

# 7

# Repentance and Conversion

On the inside of the Beautiful Gate in the Portico of Solomon, Peter models prophetic proclamation that invites response. He exposes his audience's rejection of their savior, and complicity in the killing of Jesus, and proclaims God's raising him from the dead. He declares that the healing is done in the name of Jesus, the people's crucified and risen Messiah. He then offers a word of grace followed by a call to repentance, conversion, and recruitment for mission.

Before awaiting any kind of visible response from his audience after his hard-hitting exposé of their crimes against Jesus, he offers a surprising declaration of grace: "And now, brethren, I know that you acted in ignorance, just as your rulers did also" (Acts 3:17). He echoes Jesus' words from the cross: "Father, forgive them; for they do not know what they are doing," without excusing their actions as inconsequential (Luke 23:33). God's mercy and love are the priority emphasis—the divine kindness that leads to repentance (Rom. 2:4). Peter, like Jesus, forgives their guilt before they confess (Luke 5:20; 7:47).

On the last day of a training we offered to pastors and leaders in Siberia, Russia, we were was asked to pray individually for eighteen men in a recovery house. We divided into two teams. Mériadek, a French banker fluent in Russian, and I began to pray for the first person who stepped forward from amongst the men who lined up along a wall of the house. The man appeared to be in his fifties. The deep lines on his face revealed hard living and untold suffering. Due to time constraints, we didn't ask any questions other than his name, and I began to pray, with Mériadek interpreting.

An impression came to me that I was to speak over his hands, that Jesus was cleansing them of the blood, and to tell him that Jesus forgives all his sins. Without analyzing, I began by asking him if I could pray for his hands. He lifted up his massive palms, lined like his face. I spoke out my impressions, telling him: "Jesus forgives you for all your sins and cleanses your hands of the blood. In the name of Jesus, I silence all voices of accusation and lift off all guilt."

As soon as Mériadek's Russian version of my words reached his ears, the man began shaking and fell backwards, while Mériadek and I quickly positioned ourselves to ease him down. We continued to pray over his heart, affirming that God had made him for compassion, was softening the hard places, and resurrecting the dead ones. The man's eyes remained closed and he moved his head from side-to-side, visibly touched. Once we were done praying, some men helped him up, and we began praying for the next guy. Each of the men seemed deeply moved by the prayer. After two hours or so we had prayed for all the men as well as the pastors who accompanied us.

Upon returning to our host Andrey's apartment, he told us that the first man we prayed for had been part of the most elite special-forces battalion of the Russian military in Afghanistan. He had participated in massacres of Afghan villagers during raids, killing many. Upon returning home to Siberia after the war, he learned that his niece was raped, and planned his vengeance on the perpetrators. Before this could happen, though, the rapist and two other men attacked him with axes in the middle of the night while he was sleeping. He reputedly killed all three men with an axe before turning himself into to the local police, and was sentenced to eighteen years in prison, where he killed two others. Through prophetic prayer in the flow of the name of Jesus, we experienced the kindness of God as grace and forgiveness washing over this man, as he was refreshed by the Holy Spirit.

In Acts 3, we are not told many details regarding the physical or emotional impact of Peter's proclamation on his listeners, other than that about 5,000 men believed the message they heard. We are, however, given a lot of important details regarding the content of Peter's proclamation.

Peter places his denunciation of his audience's actions against Jesus into the broader perspective of God's plan of salvation through redemptive suffering, stating: "But the things which God announced beforehand by the mouth of all the prophets, that His Christ would suffer, he has thus fulfilled" (Acts 3:18). Here the writer of Acts brilliantly inserts early Christian interpretation of Jesus as Israel's conquering Messiah who wins by losing, conquering death through his own death and resurrection within a larger Old Testament prophetic tradition. Peter boldly states that the suffering Messiah whom the people kill was announced by all the prophets—as we have seen in chapter five. Yet the people's ignorance and God's plan do not negate their responsibility.

Peter does not stop by publically recognizing the ignorance of the people and their rulers in their participation in killing Jesus. Nor does he end his preaching by stating that what happened to Jesus was announced beforehand and had to happen, excusing them still further. Peter calls his listeners to respond to his message by confessing, repenting, and turning around: "Therefore repent and return, so that your sins may be wiped away, in order that times of refreshing may come from the presence of the Lord" (Acts 3:19).

## BAPTISM OF REPENTANCE FOR THE FORGIVENESS OF SINS

A change of mind and turn around are needed so that people's sins will be wiped out. The wiping away of sin has been accomplished by Jesus through his death and resurrection. However, potential beneficiaries must appropriate this provision through turning to Jesus in repentance and conversion by faith. Peter's preaching here is an embodiment of the central mission of Luke and Acts: the invitation into the baptism of repentance for the forgiveness of sins.

In Luke's Gospel, John the Baptist first preached this baptism (Luke 3:3). Jesus gave special attention to society's outcasts, tax collectors, and sinners, and yet also called them to repentance. "I have not come to call the righteous but sinners to repentance" (Luke 5:32). Jesus describes the repentance of sinners enthusiastically: "I tell you, there will be more joy in heaven over one sinner who repents than over ninety-nine righteous persons who need no repentance" (Luke 15:7). In his parable of the Pharisee and the publican, Jesus presents the Pharisee as standing in the temple, praying to himself, "God, I thank you that I am not like other people: swindlers, unjust, adulterers, or even like this tax collector. I fast twice a week; I pay tithes of all that I get" (Luke 18:11-12). Jesus elevates the repentant tax collector, who stands in the back, unwilling to lift his eyes to heaven, beating his breast and saying, "God be merciful to me, the sinner." This phrase was attached to the invocation of the name of Jesus by the early church fathers as an essential posture in ceaseless prayer. "This one went to his house justified rather than the other," says Jesus, in one of his many critiques of the highly religious Pharisees (Luke 18:14).

Finally, Jesus interprets his mission to his disciples when he appears to them after his resurrection: "Thus it is written, that the Christ would suffer and rise again from the dead the third day, and that repentance for forgiveness of sins would be proclaimed in his name to all the nations, beginning from Jerusalem. You are witnesses of these things" (Luke 24:45-47).

## REPENTANCE AND CONVERSION

But what, exactly does it mean to repent and turn? How do these two actions differ and compliment each other? Street-level understandings of repentance almost always include the expression of heartfelt sorrow or contrition for wrongdoing, such as the tax collector in the temple who beat his chest. However, the word "repent" (*metanoeo*) or "repentance" (*metanoia*) literally means to have an "after" or "exchanged" (*meta*)[1] mind (*nous*).[2] Repent, then, means to change one's perception or understanding so that it is in alignment with what the Holy Spirit helps us to see about God's love for us and what needs to change in our lives. Zaccheus responds to Jesus' inviting himself over to his house with a gesture of repentance: "Behold, Lord, half of my possessions I will give to the poor, and if I have defrauded anyone of anything, I will give back four times as much" (Luke 19:8).

Peter's imperative, "turn," comes from the Greek verb *epistrepho*, which means to return, turn around, or be converted. Turning is best understood relationally, as turning around to face and move towards God revealed in Jesus. Being in relationship with God includes speaking to God through prayer and tuning in to hear God speaking to us.[3] It was prophesied over John the Baptist that he would "turn many of the sons of Israel back to the Lord their God" (Luke 1:16). This turning means a relationship with the living God rather than following laws or religious tradition. Peter models a new level of the prophetic vocation embodied by John the Baptist, which continues now in this period between Jesus' first and second comings. Forerunners, such as Peter, are needed to speak out before Christ's return: "in the spirit and power of Elijah, to turn the hearts of the fathers back to the

---

1. *Meta* in composition means "exchange, transfer, transmutation," or can mean "after." See Joseph Henry Thayer, *Thayer's Greek-English Lexicon of the New Testament* (New York: Harper & Brothers, 1889), Accordance Bible Software, 3326, III.2.

2. *Nous* refers to "the psychological faculty of understanding, reasoning, thinking, and deciding" (J. P. Louw and Eugene Albert Nida, eds., "Nous," in *Greek-English Lexicon of the New Testament*, Accordance Bible Software, 26.14), or "the mind, comprising alike the faculties of perceiving and understanding and those of feeling, judging, determining; hence, specifically, the intellective faculty, the understanding" (Thayer, 3563.1).

3. See the Septuagint of Deut. 6:1-10.

children, and the disobedient to the attitude of the righteous, so as to make ready a people prepared for the Lord" (Luke 1:17).

Believing in and turning towards are intimately linked. When unnamed disciples, scattered due to the persecution in connection with Stephen, preached the Lord Jesus to the Greeks, "large numbers . . . believed and turned to the Lord" (Acts 11:21).

When Paul preaches to the Gentiles in Lystra, he calls them to turn away from worshipping and sacrificing to Greek gods Zeus and Hermes, which he calls "these vain things," and invites them to "turn to the living God" (Acts 14:15). Paul describes the resurrected Jesus whom he encountered on the road to Damascus. Jesus told Paul that he was rescuing him from the Jews and Gentiles "to open their eyes so that they may turn from darkness to light and from the dominion of Satan to God, that they may receive forgiveness of sins and an inheritance among those who have been sanctified by faith in me" (Acts 26:18).

## RECEIVING THE PROMISE OF THE FATHER

Jesus also emphasized the need for the Holy Spirit to fill and empower his followers to bear witness to him. He calls this the "promise of the Father," saying: "And behold, I am sending forth the promise [epaggelia] of my Father upon you; but you are to stay in the city until you are clothed with power from on high" (Luke 24:48-49). Right before he ascends to the Father, Jesus re-emphasizes the disciples' need to await an event of empowerment by the Spirit to proclaim repentance for the forgiveness of sins to the nations. Jesus knew that the mission he himself embodied included resistance from the powers and great suffering, which is why he so urgently insisted that they wait for the promised Holy Spirit.

> He commanded them not to leave Jerusalem, but to wait for what the Father had promised [epaggelia], "Which," he said, "you heard of from me; for John baptized with water, but you will be baptized with the Holy Spirit not many days from now." (Acts 1:4-5)

The Holy Spirit comes on the day of Pentecost in fulfillment of Jesus' words, filling all the gathered believers. A tongue of fire appears and rests on each individual. Those filled with the Spirit are enabled to speak in tongues, which are spoken languages recognized by visitors to Jerusalem from many nations. Jews and proselytes alike are amazed and greatly perplexed, asking, "How is it that we each hear them in our own language to which we were born? ... We hear them in our own tongues speaking of the mighty deeds of God" (Acts 2:9, 11).

Peter himself is empowered with new boldness with the Spirit upon him. In Peter's first sermon during the immediate aftermath, he emphasizes Jesus' exaltation "to the right hand of God," where he himself "received from the Father the promise of the Holy Spirit poured forth this which you both see and hear" (Acts 2:33). Much like in his sermon at the Portico of Solomon, Peter's first sermon after Pentecost emphasizes repentance, the baptism of repentance for the forgiveness of sins, and receiving of the gift of the Holy Spirit.

> Repent, and each of you be baptized in the name of Jesus Christ for the forgiveness of your sins; and you will receive the gift of the Holy Spirit. For the promise is for you and your children and for all who are far off, as many as the Lord our God will call to Himself. (Acts 2:38-39)

## BAPTISM OF THE SPIRIT IN MOZAMBIQUE

On the last day of a ten-day trip to Mozambique, I was teaching pastors in a school run by Iris Ministries in Pemba. Heidi Baker, the founding missionary, came to me hours before my flight, asking me to help her pray for the pastors to receive the baptism of the Holy Spirit. Heidi assured me that she'd get me and my then thirteen-year-old daughter, Anna, to our flight. I was intrigued how an experienced Pentecostal pastor such as Heidi would bring people into this highly valued experience of God.

Heidi and I walked across the red sand to the covered areas where 200 or so men were gathered for a class. Heidi spoke to them about the need to first repent, inviting the Holy Spirit to search their hearts to reveal anything that needed to be confessed and turned away from. Most of the pastors immediately got down on their knees, confessing their sins. After this, Heidi invited them to posture themselves as if they were about to receive a gift. Most of the people extended their hands, and Heidi and I went around, laying our hands on and praying for each person. Many began speaking in languages that sounded different than Makhuwa or Portuguese. Others prayed and continued to wait. At the end, Heidi debriefed the group, asking what they'd experienced.

"I saw a man come to me dressed in all white," one man recounted. "He told me it was good that I am here," he continued, grinning broadly.

## BAPTISM IN THE SPIRIT IN WASHINGTON STATE REFORMATORY

The Sunday after the American public elected Donald Trump as President, my colleague Mike and I met with six Mexican immigrants incarcerated in Washington State Reformatory. All but two of the men were either undocumented immigrants or legal permanent residents who will be directly affected by Donald Trump's promise to deport immigrants who have committed crimes (labeled by US immigration law as "criminal aliens").

We began singing worship songs together. We felt the refreshing presence of God upon us, bringing palpable joy and comfort. We read together Jesus' words regarding the impending destruction of the temple in Jerusalem in Luke 21:5-19, with his alerts that false saviors will come, nation will rise against nation, and natural disasters such as earthquakes, plagues, and famines will occur. We were all struck by Jesus' first warning: "See to it that you are not misled; for many will come in my name, saying, 'I am he,' and, 'The time is near.' Do not go after them" (Luke 21:8).

We discussed the natural tendency to fear and the temptation to go after strong leaders who sound like they have it together. In the prison context, these words sound especially comforting, as incarcerated people are unable to respond to world events. Whether they are immigrants or US citizens, as inmates they cannot vote, enlist, or organize. They can and do become disturbed and fearful as they feel especially out of control and unable to protect their loved ones. Jesus' words here can be put into practice by them: "When you hear of wars and disturbances, do not be terrified; for these things must take place first, but the end does not follow immediately" (Luke 21:9).

Jesus warns that, before the end, believers will experience persecution. We read Luke 21:12 together: "They will lay their hands on you and will persecute you, delivering you to the synagogues and prisons, bringing you before kings and governors for my name's sake."

Since the men have already survived their arrests and are currently imprisoned, they already know what might be involved in enduring this higher calling of persecution for Jesus' name. Following Jesus in the prison setting is not easy. "People ignore us or mock us and put us down for getting religious once we're in trouble but not seeking God on the outside when things are good," one of them remarks. "When you're in prison and you go to church a lot, people accuse you of being a *rapo*.[4] They shut you out of their circles," another inmate adds.

The men are encouraged by Jesus' words that give meaning, purpose, and a hope-filled strategy to all who are persecuted. As new believers experiencing persecution for righteousness sake inside the prison system, these words include them, and deeply inspire and encourage.

> It will lead to an opportunity for your testimony. So make up your minds not to prepare beforehand to defend yourselves; for I will give you utterance and

---

4. A "rapo" is anyone convicted of a sex crime, a status highly despised by inmates. Prisoners who attend lots of religious services are sometimes falsely labeled "rapos" or "chi-mos" (child molesters) as a form of persecution.

wisdom which none of your opponents will be able to
resist or refute. (Luke 21:14-15)

Jesus does not prophesy a safe and successful future for
his followers. He does not set those facing hardship or rejection
up for disappointment. Rather, Jesus describes a road forward
marked by increased adversity and hope.

> But you will be betrayed even by parents and brothers
> and relatives and friends, and they will put some of you
> to death, and you will be hated by all because of my
> name. Yet not a hair of your head will perish. By your
> endurance you will gain your lives. (Luke 21:16-19)

Endurance is exactly what those serving time in our prison
system need. I am inspired to witness these men soak up Jesus'
teaching like thirsty plants in a drought.

Jesus does not call his followers to fight to protect his Jewish homeland, nor even the holy city of Jerusalem. The inmates
could not do this even if they wanted to. Even the holy city will
"fall by the edge of the sword, and will be led captive into all the
nations; and Jerusalem will be trampled under foot by the Gentiles until the times of the Gentiles are fulfilled" (Luke 21:24). No
one and no place is immune to coming turmoil.

We discuss how now we are perhaps still in "the time of the
Gentiles," the period between Jesus' first and second comings,
when Jesus calls his disciples to "make disciples of all nations,
baptizing them in the name of the Father, the Son and the Holy
Spirit" (Matt. 28:18-20). If Jerusalem is not to be defended, how
much less should followers of Jesus be concerned with homeland
defense of any other nation? For men who are unable to defend
their families or nation due to incarceration, Jesus' words still include them, offering a way forward with clear spiritual practices.

In Jesus' end-time scenario, there is no place for fighting or
for denying coming difficulties. Rather, Jesus offers an opened-
eyed realism which, at the same time, inspires hope in the face of
the most terrifying events.

> There will be signs in sun and moon and stars, and on the earth dismay among nations, in perplexity at the roaring of the sea and the waves, men fainting from fear and the expectation of the things which are coming upon the world; for the powers of the heavens will be shaken. Then they will see the Son of Man coming in a cloud with power and great glory. (Luke 21:25-27)

"The worse things get, the closer we get to the best news possible—Jesus' arrival to make all things new," I say. This is yet another example that sin and chaos do not separate God from us. As Paul affirms, "where sin increased, grace abounded all the more" (Rom. 5:20).

I briefly describe how the shaking of the powers of the heavens refers directly to God's judgment of the invisible rulers, authorities, and powers that underlie the visible powers of nations, prisons, and all organizations. This preview encourages people whose futures seem sealed by sentences and policies that dim hopes of clemency or parole. Does it encourage you? If not, why not?

For people serving long prison sentences, only an act of God will shift the foundations, like the shaking open of prison doors and shackles in Acts 16 (which we will consider in the next chapter). Jesus himself must come, and he will. This is the only solution that will make any real difference for people serving long or life sentences, deportation, and other big challenges. In the face of growing global chaos, Jesus commands his followers: "But when these things begin to take place, straighten up and lift up your heads, because your redemption is drawing near" (Luke 21:28).

I invite the men to take Jesus' words seriously now. "Let's straighten up, lift up our heads, and refuse the shaming, humiliating gaze and the crushing effects of punishment," I say. I watch the men as they adjust themselves in their plastic chairs, straightening their posture and lifting their heads. Faint smiles appearing on some of their faces. Finally we read Luke 21:34-36:

> Be on guard, so that your hearts will not be weighted down with dissipation and drunkenness and the

worries of life, and that day will not come on you suddenly like a trap; for it will come upon all those who
dwell on the face of all the earth. But keep on the alert
at all times, praying that you may have strength to escape all these things that are about to take place, and to
stand before the Son of Man.

Here Jesus warns that the day will come on "all who dwell
on the face of the earth," not just on the less fortunate or those
viewed as deserving punishment. Once again, Jesus' final commands are possible for anyone, including inmates, to practice.
"Be on guard," and, "keep on the alert at all times, praying," are
actions that are necessary for prisoners watching their backs for
predators or enemies. Yet the focus here is on avoiding being
weighed down by drugs, alcohol, and worries, and on receiving
strength to endure to the end.

Rogelio, an inmate serving a 555-month sentence, speaks
clearly and confidently to his fellow inmates, "You know, it is
important that we urge our family members to know where they
stand before God. This life is short and it is not our final destina-
tion. We must challenge our family members to be reconciled
with God." He then shared how his sister had just told him
during a recent trailer visit with his family[5] how she had been
deeply touched by the Holy Spirit while praying, and had begun
to speak in another language. "There's more [of God] available to
all of us," he said, "and we must be open."

At this point I remember the Mozambican pastors kneel-
ing in the dirt at the Iris Global base in Pemba, confessing their
sins before receiving the baptism of the Holy Spirit. I share this
memory with them, telling them that I am feeling inspired at
this moment to confess my sins and ask Jesus to fill me with
the Holy Spirit afresh. I ask them if they would like to join me
in confessing our sins and ask the Spirit to fill us and empower
us to follow Jesus in prison. I explain that, along with the Holy

5. A "trailer visit" is a scheduled period in which an inmate of a prison
or jail is permitted to spend several hours or days in private with a visitor,
usually their legal spouse.

Spirit, we receive spiritual gifs, such as wisdom, prophesy, healing, and speaking in tongues. Boldness to share the good news
with others is also a valuable fruit of Spirit empowerment, I add.

Everyone nods their heads, and there's enthusiastic agreement to pray. I kneel down in front of my chair there in the prison chapel, but clarify that people should only do what they feel
comfortable doing. Each man kneels, and we confess together
for a while before Mike and I go around and lay hands on each
one, praying for the filling of the Holy Spirit. Rogelio gets up after
we pray and lays hands on Mike and me as well, praying for us
to be filled. The men look refreshed as the hour approaches for
"inmate movement," when everyone must be at the door of the
chapel to head back to their cells for the afternoon count. I feel
the buzz of God's Spirit upon me and am delighted when Steve, a
Chicano man from Texas says, "Thank you! I am so glad I came.
I never expected this would be so encouraging and refreshing."

Peter calls his listeners to repentance and conversion, offering as incentive the forgiveness of sins, refreshing in the Holy
Spirit, and God's sending of Jesus himself to them in a future
(second) coming. Peter speaks in alignment with his master, Jesus. He urges his listeners to respond in ways that go beyond my
normal comfort level, insisting that these actions are essential in
order "that he [God] may send Jesus, the Christ appointed for
you" (Acts 3:20).

## THE COMINGS OF THE MESSIAH

Peter presents an understanding of the coming of the Christ that
divides Old Testament prophesies about the coming of Israel's
Messiah into two distinct comings. First, in keeping with his the
ology of the cross, Peter presents Jesus as the suffering Messiah
who came, not to restore Israel, but to save the world through the
rejection of his own people and his agony on the cross. Second,
and still in the future, Peter presents Jesus as returning in judgment and restoration, as foretold by the prophets, "all the prophets who have spoken, from Samuel and his successors onward,

also announced these days" (Acts 3:25). Peter preaches Jesus "whom heaven must receive until the period of restoration of all things about which God spoke by the mouth of His holy prophets from ancient time" (Acts 3:21).

Jesus' disciples asked him directly, "Lord, is it at this time you are restoring the kingdom to Israel?" (Acts 1:6). Jesus prohibits special knowledge for his disciples then and now. "It is not for you to know times or epochs which the Father has fixed by his own authority" (Acts 1:7). Jesus refocuses his followers' attention onto the highest priorities between his first and second comings. "But you will receive power when the Holy Spirit has come upon you; and you shall be my witnesses both in Jerusalem, and in all Judea and Samaria, and even to the remotest part of the earth" (Acts 1:8). May we continue to realign our focus to Jesus' priorities, resisting the temptations to align with the defense of nation states! In alignment with Jesus, Peter says nothing about the restoration of Israel. Instead, he calls his Jewish listeners to follow their Messiah Jesus' teachings, recruiting them into the new and final period of Israel, and the world's, history.

Peter puts fire in his message, drawing from scripture passages that held great authority for his Jewish audience. He quotes Moses, his people's highest authority, warning his listeners of the urgency of paying attention: "Moses said, 'the Lord God will raise up for you a prophet like me from your brethren; to him you shall give heed to everything he says to you [Deut. 18:18-19]. And it will be that every soul that does not heed that prophet shall be utterly destroyed from among the people'" (Acts 3:22-23; cf. Lev. 23:29).

Peter offers no alternative but to fully heed Jesus as the Prophet Moses foresaw, warning of disastrous consequences should his gathered listeners ignore their Messiah. Jesus had already prophesied the destruction of the very temple where they were then gathered. But being "utterly destroyed from among the people" is certainly grave. This is a direct citation from the Septuagint of Leviticus 23:29, which refers to people being cut off or destroyed[6] who do not humble themselves on the Day of Atonement, when the people's sins are confessed and atoned for through sacrifice and priestly intercession.[7] Peter links Jesus' identity as prophet to his identity as Savior who atones for humanity's sins. However, his emphasis is on the people who are now listening to the resurrected Jesus, that they might step into their missionary vocation to the nations. Peter shows a willingness to turn up the heat on his compatriots in a way that pushes many of us beyond our comfort levels. He commends the urgency of proclaiming Jesus now. So why does he do this?

## RECRUITED INTO GOD'S PEOPLE'S UNIVERSAL MISSION

Peter expresses urgency in recruiting his listeners into Israel's strongest tradition regarding universal mission, God's call of Abraham. He addresses his gathered people as "sons of the prophets," an identification linking them to Isaiah's servant/ child[8] called to carry on Israel's prophetic vocation to the nations.

> It is you who are the sons of the prophets and of the covenant which God made with your fathers, saying to Abraham, "and in your seed all the families of the earth shall be blessed." (Acts 3:24-25)[9]

6. In the Septuagint, the Greek term *exolothreuo* can signify being cut off from the people as in ex-communicated (Gen. 17:14; Exod. 12:15, 19; Lev. 17:4, 9; Num. 9:13; 15:30; 19:20). However, in the majority of cases, it refers to literal physical destruction, including death (Exod. 31:14; Lev. 18:29; Deut. 1:27; 2:34; 3:6; 4:38; 6:15; 7:4, 23, 24; 9:3, 8, 14, 19, 25; 10:10; 12:29; 18:12; 20:19-20; 28:61, 63; 31:3, 4, 19).

7. See Lev.16:29-34.

8. In the Septuagint of Isaiah, the Hebrew term *'ebed* is most often matched by the Greek term *pais*, which means child, son, or servant.

9. Peter uses language from the Septuagint of Gen. 12:3, citing parts of it word-for-word, with one interesting exception. He replaces the word used in the Septuagint, *phylē*, meaning "tribe" and often used for Gentiles (Septuagint Gen. 10:5, 18, 20; 12:3; 28:14), but also for Israel, with *patria*, meaning "family," a word more directly used to refer to Israel, with the exception of the Septuagint of Pss. 21:27 and 95:7. This supports his point to emphasize that Jesus came to bring the Jewish people into their prophetic and missional

In Isaiah. 40-55, the servant of the Lord is most often overtly referring to the people of Israel as a whole.[10] Servant Israel is described as being chosen by the Lord to bring justice to the nations and to the earth (Isa. 42:1-2, 4). "The coastlands will wait expectantly for his law" (Isa. 42:4; *torah* means teaching, in Hebrew). Servant Israel is called to be a light to the nations and to bring God's salvation to the ends of the earth (Isa. 42:6; 49:6). But how will this universal vocation be carried out when Israel herself is captive in exile, or in active rebellion against God?

Isaiah points the way forward. First, he shows that Israel's status as blind, deaf, and imprisoned does not disqualify her from this high vocation.[11] Second, Isaiah presents the Lord's servant as a singular future individual, also called "child/servant" or "slave,"[12] who goes beyond what the people as a whole could ever accomplish. This servant's unique role is most fully described is in Isaiah 52:13-53:12.[13] Here, a singular servant figure is presented as despised and rejected by the people, carrying the people's griefs and sorrows, crushed for their iniquities, which fall completely upon him (Isa. 53:4-6). He "justifies many," bearing their iniquities and sins[14] to the point of death.[15] Isaiah's prophetic oracle declares that the "good pleasure of the Lord will prosper in his hand" (Isa. 53:11). The Lord will allot this servant "a portion with the great" (Isa. 53:12). The Septuagint

---

destiny. Acts 3:25 reads, "καὶ ἐν τῷ σπέρματί σου [ἐν-]ευλογηθήσονται πᾶσαι αἱ πατριαὶ τῆς γῆς, in contrast to the Septuagint of Gen. 12:3 which reads: "καὶ ἐνευλογηθήσονται ἐν σοὶ πᾶσαι αἱ φυλαὶ τῆς γῆς."

10. Isa. 41:8, 9; 42:19; 43:10; 44:1, 2, 21, 21, 26; 45:4; 48:20; 49:3.

11. See Isa. 42:18-22. Servant Israel is depicted as embodying the people under judgment of Isa. 6:9-13, who are blind and deaf to God's word. Jesus himself sees his people as embodying the fulfillment of this passage in his time (Luke 8:10), yet they are still appealed to here as "sons of the prophets."

12. In the Septuagint of Isa. 49:3, 5, *doulos* (slave) matches *eved* (servant).

13. The servant's identity cannot be reduced to collective Israel in numerous texts (Isa. 42:1; 49:5, 6, 7; 50:10; 52:13; 53:11).

14. Isa. 53:11, 12.

15. Isa. 53:8, 9, 12.

of this oracle declares that "he will see his seed,"[16] linking this figure's descendants directly to Abraham's seed[17] through whom every family of the earth will be blessed.[18] The Apostle Paul uses this same language from the Septuagint of Genesis and Isaiah to link the seed of Abraham directly to Jesus in Galatians 3:16-17.

> Now the promises were spoken to Abraham and to his seed. He does not say, "And to seeds," as referring to many, but rather to one, "And to your seed," that is, Christ.

Paul's interpretations allow us to read Peter's recruiting call in Acts 3 to include non-Jews into Abraham's covenant. Paul argues in Galatians 3 and in Romans 4 that Gentiles are included in Abraham's spiritual heritage by faith, which "was reckoned to him as righteousness" . . . "So then those who are of faith are blessed with Abraham, the believer" (Gal. 3:6, 9). In Romans 4, Paul develops this idea further, demonstrating the inclusion of non-Jews into Abraham's covenant by grace.

> For this reason it is by faith, in order that it may be in accordance with grace, so that the promise will be guaranteed to all the descendants, not only to those who are of the Law, but also to those who are of the faith of Abraham, who is the father of us all. (Rom. 4:16)

According to numerous echoes throughout the New Testament, Jesus fulfills the people of Israel's prophetic vocation as the

---

16. Septuagint of Isa. 53:10.

17. The term "seed" used here in the Septuagint of Isa. 53:10 links Isaiah's servant's seed/descendent to the covenant God made with Abraham and the patriarchs (Gen. 12:7; 13:15; 15:5, 18; 16:10; 17:7-10, 19; 22:17-18; 24:7, 60; 26:24; 28:24). In all of these cases, the Greek term *sperma* matches the Hebrew text's *zera* (descendant). "Additionally, Ishmael, Esau, and other "not chosen" descendants (who came to be known as Gentiles too) throughout history are still from Abraham's seed. The Jews are from Israel, but there are a lot of "outsider" relatives in that lineage descended from Abraham"

18. The texts that most clearly link the promise that all the families of the earth will be blessed through Abraham's seed (*sperma*) are in Gen. 26:4 (nations, *ethnos*) and Gen. 28:14 (tribes, *phylē*).

Lord's Servant, opening the way for future descendants of Israel ("sons of the prophets") to step into Abraham's destiny to be a blessing to all nations.[19]

Jesus reads Isaiah 61:1-2 during his first public address in the synagogue of his hometown, Nazareth, stating: "The Spirit of the Lord is upon me, because he anointed me to preach the Gospel to the poor. He has sent me to proclaim release to the captives, and recovery of sight to the blind, to set free those who are oppressed, to proclaim the favorable year of the Lord" (Luke 4:18-19). "This Scripture has been fulfilled in your hearing," states Jesus, identifying himself as Isaiah's servant to the "sons of the prophets." He is the one who carries the Spirit who empowers this universal mission.

Jesus' fulfillment of these scriptures doesn't mean that there's nothing more for him (or us) to do. Jesus himself embodies the servant Israel's mission, modeling and offering liberation to Israel for their journey forward as the quintessential representative of God's missionary people in the world. Peter himself states this clearly, identifying Jesus as the Lord's Servant prophesied in Isaiah: "For you first, God raised up his Servant and sent him to bless you by turning every one of you from your wicked ways" (Acts 3:26).

Peter affirms that Jesus is the prophet Moses foretold, whom God would raise up.[20] God raised Jesus up "for you first," to liberate and empower the Jewish people so they can step into the fullness of their destiny to be a blessing to every family of the earth. Peter uses the verb "raise up" as in resurrect from the dead. Killing Jesus did not eliminate him as Israel's Savior and recruiter into universal mission. He is alive and active on the scene, as was just demonstrated by the healing at the Beautiful Gate. Peter concludes his message by emphasizing that God

19. Key New Testament passages include Matt. 12:18-21; Phil. 2:7-8. For a fuller treatment, see Ekblad, *Isaiah's Servant Poems*, 287-290.

20. The writer of Acts uses the same verb for "raise up" (*anistēmi*) regarding the prophet like Moses that God would raise up in Acts 3:22 as he uses for God's Servant (Jesus) in Acts 3:26. This verb is often used to refer to resurrection from the dead (Luke 9:8, 19; 16:31; 18:33; 24:7, 46; Acts 2:24, 32).

raised Jesus first to bless Israel, but with the objective of turning each individual away from evil so they would be available for their mission as God's servants.

Turning each person away from evil is a new and stronger emphasis than Peter's earlier call to "repent and return," which involves turning towards God. In contrast, turning away (*apostrephō*) from evil assumes the people gathered in the temple are themselves engaging in evil practices, such as participating in the crucifixion of Jesus.

The call to religious insiders themselves to turn away from evil practices evokes Israel's prophets, as in Jeremiah 25:5, "Turn ye every one from his evil way, and from your evil practices, and ye shall dwell in the land which I gave to you and your fathers, of old and for ever."[21] Peter places himself and John within the prophetic stream featured in Jeremiah 42:15.[22]

> And I sent to you my servants the prophets, saying, Turn ye every one from his evil way, and amend your practices, and go not after other gods to serve them, and ye shall dwell upon the land which I gave to you and to your fathers: but ye inclined not your ears, your fathers: but ye inclined not your ears, and hearkened not.[23]

In this period between Pentecost and Jesus' second coming, we too must call Christians and others on the inside of the *beautiful gate* to renounce allegiances to false gods and sever unhealthy attachments, so people can become free to embody and proclaim Jesus' liberating message outside the gate.

Right as Peter's proclamation is highlighting the objective of Jesus' work to mobilize everyone there in the temple as Jesus' envoys, authorities come to arrest them. This reaction shows that the multiplication and mobilization of people of God for

21. Lancelot C. L. Brenton, trans., *Septuagint* (London: Samuel Bagster & Sons, 1851).

22. See the Septuagint of Jon. 3:8-10; Zech. 1:4; Isa. 9:12; 30:15; 42:17; Jer. 23:22; 25:5; 33:3; 43:3, 7; 51:5.

23. Brenton, *Septuagint*.

holistic transformational ministry in Jesus' name is what pro-
vokes persecution. The powers are threatened when followers of
Jesus proclaim and demonstrate Jesus' resurrected presence, the
subject of our next and final chapter.

# 8

# Persecution and Breakthrough

The first visible effect of Peter's preaching in the aftermath of the miraculous healing is his and John's arrest and imprisonment by temple authorities. Life and ministry in alignment with Jesus in the power of the Spirit leads directly to opposition from those in power, whether religious or secular. Adversaries of Jesus' Kingdom interrupt his followers in the midst of their speaking.

> As they were speaking to the people, the priests and the captain of the temple guard and the Sadducees came up to them, being greatly disturbed because they were teaching the people and proclaiming in Jesus the resurrection from the dead. And they laid hands on them and put them in jail until the next day, for it was already evening. (Acts 4:1-3)

Peter and John are experiencing similar opposition from religious authorities as Jesus encountered when he taught the people. We too, in this period before Jesus' final return to restore all things, expect the powers to oppose us as they did Jesus.

Jesus warned his followers that they would be brought before synagogues, rulers, and authorities just as he was.[1] In the temple, the scribes and the chief priests "watched him, and sent spies who pretended to be righteous, in order that they might catch him in some statement, so that they could deliver him to

---

1. See Luke 12:11, where the terms *archē* and *exousia* are used.

the rule and the authority of the governor" (Luke 20:20). Peter notes this as having been fulfilled in his sermon in Acts 3:12-17, where he includes the authorities and all the people as complicit.[2]

"But before all these things, they will lay their hands on you and will persecute you, delivering you to the synagogues and prisons, bringing you before kings and governors for my name's sake. It will lead to an opportunity for your testimony" (Luke 21:12-13).

Jesus' words find near exact fulfillment as the priests, captain of the temple guard, and Sadducees lay hands on (same word) Peter and John and put them in jail, bringing them before "their rulers and elders and scribes" the next day (Acts 4:5).

As the story progresses, categories of officials continue to be mentioned (rulers, elders, scribes)[3] but also specific individuals are named (Annas, Caiaphas, John, Alexander).

> On the next day, their rulers and elders and scribes were gathered together in Jerusalem; and Annas the high priest was there, and Caiaphas and John and Alexander, and all who were of high-priestly descent. (Acts 4:5-6)

The vocabulary here begins with the notorious word "ruler," *arche* in Greek. In the Septuagint, the Gospels, and Acts, *arche* almost always designates actual governing authorities and leaders. In contrast, Paul uses these terms to designate the spiritual aspects of power and authority underlying human systems that are often presented as rebellious.

> For our struggle is not against flesh and blood, but against the rulers, against the powers, against the world forces of this darkness, against the spiritual *forces* of wickedness in the heavenly places. (Eph. 6:12)

2. See earlier discussion on Acts 3:13, pages 109-112.

3. Rulers (ἄρχοντας), elders (πρεσβυτέρους), and scribes (γραμματεῖς) are distinguished. Other titles that fit into the category of the powers include the priests, the *stratēgos*, captain (ὁ στρατηγὸς), of the temple guard, and Sadducees. Places include the sacred place (*hieron*).

In the Gospels and Acts, the rulers, authorities, and other named groups, such as Pharisees, Sadducees, scribes, priests, high priest, and places (synagogues, temples) are usually resistant or outright antagonistic towards Jesus, and are most often described without mentioning the names of individual people.[4] The categories of "the people" and "the crowd" are presented as influenced by either Jesus or the adversarial leaders. Jesus engages with his adversaries, responding to their questions, and challenging them in ways that are consistent with Paul's understanding that everything is under the sovereignty of God, and called to recognize and serve Jesus and his Kingdom purposes.

> By him [Christ] all things were created, both in the heavens and on earth, visible and invisible, whether thrones or dominions or rulers or authorities—all things have been created through him and for him. He is before all things, and in Him all things hold together. (Col. 1:16-17)

Jesus is presented in Colossians 2:10 as "the head over all rule and authority"—an emphasis strongly stated elsewhere, as in Ephesians 1:20-23, where Paul writes that God "raised him from the dead and seated him at his right hand in the heavenly places, far above all rule and authority and power and dominion, and every name that is named, not only in this age but also in the one to come. And he put all things in subjection under his feet, and gave Him as head over all things to the church, which is his body, the fullness of him who fills all in all."

These first apostles understood the rebellious nature of the powers, experiencing accusations, arrests, beatings, incarceration, and martyrdom at their hands. Their realism and boldness are desperately needed by today's Christians, who are often overly beholden to powers both secular and religious, and prone to justify and defend them. We, too often, encounter this rebellious state of the powers in our advocacy with people going through our court system.

4. This contrasts with other characters, such as the disciples or people who come to Jesus for help, who are often named.

Skagit County Superior Court has implemented two pre-disposition therapeutic courts for offenders who meet the requirements and are admitted: Mental Health Court and Drug Court. Felony charges and prison sentences are deferred for people charged with crimes proven to have been influenced by treatable mental health disorders or substance abuse issues. Those accepted into these programs are released and required to comply with strict guidelines, including receiving regular counseling, participating in treatment programs, twelve-step groups, and the like. Random urine analyses (UAs) to detect drug or alcohol consumption and weekly fees to cover supervision costs are all part of a demanding program monitored by regular court appearances. The threat of conviction and prison sentence is always looming, and shorter stints in jail are used as sanctions by the therapeutic courts to drive the point home. When accompanying people pastorally who are under the supervision of mental health or drug court, it is critical that Christian advocates side with the person rather than the State. This is equally true when accompanying people on probation.

Washington State's Department of Corrections (DOC) typically keeps people released from prison sentences under probation for periods of time ranging from one to several years. Men and women coming out of prison have a myriad of pressures upon release, including finding housing and employment with the label "felon" or "ex-con," paying off fines that have gone into collection, getting driver licenses re-issued (that have been suspended due to driving infractions or not paying child support or fines), and re-connecting with estranged family members, especially children. Probation officers require regular check-ins during business hours, interrupting ex-prisoners' work schedules (if they have a job), and requiring travel (they often are without valid driver licenses or means of transportation).

Ex-prisoners often have a level of resentment towards the State for requiring post-release supervision, which is technically part of their prison sentence. People often miss these appointments, triggering further imprisonment. Increasingly, ex-prisoners are being charged by the DOC with "escape," and subsequently pursued by heavily-armed authorities who function as bounty hunters.

I have accompanied a man named Jeff since I met him in Skagit County Jail in late 1994, when he was charged for participating in a drive-by shooting. He went to prison at that time for several years, and has since done other prison sentences. Jeff, a Caucasian man who grew up on the streets of Skagit County, was unofficially adopted into the homes of Mexican immigrant youth as a young teenager. Jeff became involved in gangs along the way and began dealing drugs. These activities led to arrests that landed him in the juvenile detention system, Skagit County Jail, and eventually the Washington State prison system. I have pursued him consistently over more than twenty years, reading the Bible and praying with him when he's been in jail, keeping tabs on him when he's on the outs, and responding to his occasional pursuits of me during times of crisis. I have often felt like a kind of Kingdom of God bounty hunter, and Jeff says he has greatly appreciated it. "You are like a dad to me, Bob," he told me recently through the glass in the jail's visiting booth.

Jeff was most recently released over two years ago from the day of this writing. He used Tierra Nueva's address as his release address, as he had planned to go through our recovery program that was based in the building at that time. Financial and family pressures soon got the best of him, and he decided to return to a business he knew well, that had recently become legal: growing marijuana. At the same time, he blew off the DOC, missing his meetings and ignoring the threats of sanctions. Heavily-armed DOC agents surrounded Tierra Nueva looking for him, and he managed to elude law enforcement for nearly two years since then. The DOC charged him with "escape," and began pursuing him in earnest. Jeff owned a number of cars that he made sure were registered in the names of friends who didn't have active arrest warrants. He maintained his grow operations and stayed in close contact with his daughter, keeping out of more dangerous pursuits of the past. I learned the places he frequented, and we found ways to meet up to talk and pray together.

Jeff's girlfriend relapsed into her heroin addiction, giving birth to their baby in the local hospital. The hospital then alerted Child Protective Services, who put a hold on the newborn. The infant needed special medical attention due to the heroin in his system. Jeff reached out to me, saying he wanted to turn himself into the DOC and comply so he could get custody of his son. He was afraid that the escape charge might carry a serious sentence. I offered to make contact with the DOC to find out about this charge and facilitate his turning himself in.

I talked with a clerk at the front desk of the DOC and learned that the local director had been increasingly filing escape charges on people like Jeff with the Skagit County Prosecutor. I was informed that I would have to talk personally with the director about his case. A law enforcement officer in a green uniform, bullet proof vest, and big badge came out the door at that moment, and I asked her the name and phone number of her chief so I could talk with her about Jeff's case. "Good luck," she told me, "But I wouldn't get my hopes up."

I called the head official and made an appointment to see her the next week. The day came, and I met with the chief in the DOC's waiting room. She was formal, politely shaking my hand before ushering me through the security door and into her office. She was dressed in the same green military-like uniform as the officer I'd met the week before. I took a seat in front of her at her desk and explained my relationship to Jeff and the reason for my visit. I explained my long history of accompanying Jeff as his pastor, and my opinion that he was changing for the better. I shared how Jeff wanted to turn himself in and be in full compliance with the law with the recent birth of his son. I asked the woman if she had filed an escape charge and, if so, how long the standard sentences were, and whether she would consider using her discretion to withdraw the charge.

She wouldn't confirm that she had filed an escape charge, claimed ignorance regarding standard sentences for escape, and refused to respond to my request to consider using her discretion to withdraw the charge. Since I had been informed by other officials, I decided to tell her that I already knew she had, in fact, filed the charge, and asked if she would please consider withdrawing it if Jeff turned himself in that same day.

"If you are trying to negotiate something for Jeff, I can assure you that there will be no negotiating," the woman replied sternly. "Tell Mr. Peters that his only option is that he turn himself in."

I told her that I was in full favor of Jeff's compliance with DOC, and only wanted to make it easier for him and them so he would turn himself in. She looked at me suspiciously and asked if I was aware of any criminal activity he was engaged in currently. I told her that I knew about his past activities but didn't think he was involved in any current criminal activity, though I couldn't guarantee it. She asked me if I knew where he was. I responded that while I saw him from time to time, I didn't know where he was living. At this point she glared at me and spoke threateningly, evoking another law to intimidate me.

"Listen, Mr. Ekblad, if you know of Mr. Peter's whereabouts, we could have you arrested for aiding and abetting a fugitive. You are taking a big risk and we could charge you."

I looked her in the eyes and surprised myself by both my boldness and by the anger that was rising up inside.

"Don't threaten me," I told her. "I have been pastoring people like Jeff for twenty-two years. I know the laws, my rights, and my responsibilities. So do not try to intimidate me."

She stood up and pointed to the door and said in a commanding voice: "This meeting is over. It's time for you to leave my office now."

"Gladly," I replied, stood up calmly, left the room, and began walking down the hall past other offices, the official following closely behind. Right before leaving through the security door I turned and added: "I am sorry that you won't show mercy, that your heart has become so hard."

I think back to Peter and John, when the rulers summon them and prohibit them from speaking ever again in the name of Jesus. While the parallel is not direct, followers of Jesus today must not be intimidated by authorities from carrying out their roles as pastoral advocates, and certainly not any other role that the Spirit has called us into. Peter and John respond with boldness: "Whether it is right in the sight of God to give heed to you rather than to God, you be the judge; for we cannot stop speaking about what we have seen and heard" (Acts 4:18-20). The authorities respond with further threats, but have no legal basis to detain them (Acts 4:21).

Once out in the waiting room, my heart was pounding. I could feel a bit of the rage and powerlessness that ex-prisoners must feel as they deal with harsh state officials. Just then, a young, heavily-tatted man whom I knew from the jail came in from the street for his appointment. He smiled, glad to see me, and my heart was warmed.

I called Jeff as I drove away and reported my conversation to him, telling him I hoped I didn't make things worse for him. I warned him to be sure to keep his hands in the air if they eventually catch him.

"Don't give them any excuse to pull the trigger," I warned.

"Wow, Bob, thanks so much for all you do for me. That's amazing! I don't think it will get me into any more trouble than I'm already in. And I'll be careful for sure," he said.

Scripture presents the powers as having been disarmed at the cross, where Jesus "made a public display of them, having triumphed over them through him" (Col. 2:15). For me, this means that while I must treat human beings in office with honor and respect, which I'm not sure I did in my past example, I must also remember that we are on the winning side, as these powers are subject to Christ. Human representatives of the powers, such as this DOC chief, clearly are not aware that the law enforcement protocols and policies they adhere to are also under Jesus and his followers. Peter himself writes similarly about the powers' subjection to Jesus, "who is at the right hand of God, having gone into heaven, after angels and authorities and powers had been subjected to him" (1 Pet. 3:22).

In our story, Peter and John let hands be laid on them and accept being jailed. Peter appears to be practicing his own advice, "Submit yourselves for the Lord's sake to every human institution, whether to a king as the one in authority, or to governors as sent by him for the punishment of evildoers and the praise of those who do right. For such is the will of God that by doing right you may silence the ignorance of foolish men" (1 Pet. 2:13-15). At the same time, we see the apostles exercising tremendous freedom to resist the authorities' orders whenever these orders directly counter their ministry priorities, even immediately upon release from custody.

In Jeff's case, I advised him to submit to the authorities rather than continue to resist as a fugitive. However, he continued to elude the DOC for the next six months, practicing his own kind of freedom and futile resistance until he was finally caught and sent back to prison for a month-long penalty. He told me that he found himself suddenly surrounded by officers from the FBI, DOC, and local law enforcement, all with guns aimed at him.

"I remembered your words which I always take as coming from God, Bob. I grabbed my dog with both arms so they could see I couldn't reach for anything else. To tell you the truth, Bob, I am relieved to finally have been caught," he told me through the glass in Skagit County Jail's visiting booth.

He was placed in solitary confinement cell and saddled with drug charges that could send him away for as long as 120 months. Within weeks, he was transferred into one of the segregated pods within the jail which houses gang-involved inmates, officially labeled a "Security Threat Group" (STG).

For a number of years now, our local jail has housed gang-involved inmates in segregated pods to avoid run-ins with enemy gang members. At times, though, the normal stresses of incarceration combine with internal tensions within a gang, leading to fights between fellow gang members. For nearly four months this summer and fall, inmates from one particular gang were locked down, often three to a cell 24/7, as a deterrent and punishment for fighting.

During these months, they did not benefit from weekly Bible studies, nor daily time out of their cells for recreation and meals. Shortly after Jeff was transferred into this pod, where he has a lot of influence with fellow gang members, one of the sergeants was able to come to an agreement with the gang through Jeff for them to not fight one another in order to be released from their prolonged lockdown. This led to their first Bible study out of lockdown the following Thursday—a thirty-minute gathering that was a precious taste of the Kingdom of God.

Nearly the entire inmate population of the upper tier of the pod that housed these men attended our first Thursday night gathering in four months. Fifteen or so guys shuffled in and took their seats on blue plastic chairs around our familiar circle. Many of these men I'd known for years, including Jeff, whose friendship with me helped inmates I didn't yet know trust me immediately. My Tierra Nueva colleague, Matt, and I made the rounds, shaking everyone's hand, warmly welcoming them before we formally began our meeting with a prayer.

I talked directly about their official label as an STG. I invited them to look at how Jesus and his disciples were also considered an STG—leveraging their persecuted status to establish a link with the homies.

"Check this out, you guys. Jesus himself was rejected and given the death penalty by the authorities who considered him a security threat. Peter confronts the people about this in Acts 3:13-15, right when he's got their full attention after a man lame from birth has just been healed. Can someone read these verses for us?" I ask.

> God glorified his servant Jesus, the one whom you delivered over and disowned in the presence of Pilate, when he had decided to release him," one of the men reads. "But you disowned the Holy and Righteous One and asked for a murderer to be granted to you, but put to death the Prince of life, the one whom God raised from the dead, a fact to which we are witnesses. (Acts 3:13-15)

These men who've been shelved away in lockdown readily identify with the sting of rejection and the stigma of being an STG. They easily sympathize with Jesus, whom Isaiah earlier described as "despised and rejected of men, and man of sorrows and acquainted with grief" (Isa. 53:3). They are moved by God's acceptance of Jesus—the one rejected by the status quo.

At one point Jeff told the whole group how I had warned him to keep his hands in the air to keep law enforcement from an easy excuse to do away with him if they arrested him. He went on to share that one of the DOC officers who had arrested him told him as he drove him to the jail, "Too bad you didn't reach for something, because I was looking for any excuse I could find to blow you away."

I told Jeff and the others that we were glad they had all survived their arrests. They smiled and seemed heartened by my acknowledgement of these dangerous moments.

I invite the men to go against the current of the world's ongoing marginalization of Jesus, valuing him instead as the "living stone, rejected by men, but choice and precious in the sight of God" (1 Pet. 2:5). I invite them to choose to receive him who the world did not recognize and his own people didn't accept—and there is *no* resistance. We end by praying for everyone, focusing special attention on a man who sobbed as he recounted how his fifteen-year-old daughter had overdosed on heroine five days before. We prayed for this man and his family, and wrapped up with a general prayer for everyone's court cases and loved ones just as the guards pop the door open to usher the men out so the next group can be brought in.

## THE POWERS' HOSTILITY TO THE NAME

Once released from jail for preaching about Jesus, Peter and John recount to their companions all that the authorities told them regarding their hostility to Jesus' name. What they say and do reveals a lot about the nature of spiritual resistance of the powers to the Kingdom of God, and how to interpret it.

Whereas John's Gospel depicts the world in general as not recognizing Jesus, and his own people as not receiving him, the writer of Acts presents antagonism towards Jesus as coming from higher-level powers.

The gathered disciples respond to the authorities' opposition by worshipping God, affirming that he is the creator, demonstrating that they understood the powers to be under his authority.

"O Lord, it is you who made the heaven and the earth and the sea, and all that is in them," they pray, referring to the account in Genesis 1-2 of God's creation of everything (Acts 4:24). "And all that is in them" certainly includes the visible and invisible creation, as Colossians 1:16 directly states.

The disciples cite Psalm 2, a Messianic Psalm they see fulfilled not only in the powers' opposition to Jesus, but to themselves as well. They affirm the Holy Spirit's inspiration of David in his exposing of the powers' hostility to the Lord and his Christ, "Why did the gentiles rage, and the peoples devise futile things? The kings of the earth took their stand, and the rulers were gathered together against the Lord and against his Christ" (Acts 4:25-26).[5]

Different categories of powers are mentioned by name here, beginning with the nations or Gentiles (*ethnos*), the kings of the earth (*basileus tes gēs*),[6] and the rulers (*archōn*). These kings of the earth gather together,[7] in direct opposition to Jesus' mission to announce the Kingdom of God (*basileia tou theou*).[8] These powers are precisely named as the persecuted believers

---

5. The Greek New Testament cites the Septuagint of Psalm 2:1-2 word-for-word. This is the New American Standard Version's translation of the Septuagint.

6. οἱ βασιλεῖς τῆς γῆς.

7. Different players who fit within the categories of rulers and authorities "gather together" throughout the Gospels to oppose Jesus (Matt. 2:4; 22:10, 34; 26:3, 59, 27.17, 27, 63, 28.12, Luke 22.66).

8. τῆς βασιλείας τοῦ θεοῦ. See Luke 4:43; 6:20; 7:28; 8:1, 10; 9:2, 11, 27, 60; 10:9, 11; 11:20; 13:18, 20; 13:28; 16:16; 17:20; 18:16, 24, 29; 21:31; 22:29; Acts 1:3; 8:12; 19:8; 20:25; 28:23, 31.

apply this psalm to themselves. "For truly in this city there were gathered together against your holy servant Jesus, whom you anointed, both Herod and Pontius Pilate, along with the Gentiles and the peoples of Israel" (Acts 4:27-28).

Jewish and Gentile leaders Herod and Pilate, together with more inclusive categories of Gentiles and peoples of Israel, are named as having come against God's servant, Jesus, fulfilling Isaiah's prophesies about God's holy servant and anointed one.

At the same time, they see the powers as submitted to God's way of bringing about salvation through Jesus. They "do whatever your hand and your purpose predestined to occur" (Acts 4:28). These first believers do not submit to persecution as part of God's sovereignty, but as a spiritual reaction by the powers against God's sovereignty. They call on the Lord to take note of the persecution and to empower them in their resistance and in their continuation of Jesus earthly ministry of healing proclamation with signs and wonders. These early Christians intercede in ways that point the way forward to Christians now, calling on the Lord in alignment with Jesus' life. "And now, Lord, take note of their threats, and grant that your bond-servants may speak your word with all confidence, while you extend your hand to heal, and signs and wonders take place through the name of your holy servant Jesus" (Acts 4:29-30).

The people pray, and their counter-cultural gathering around Jesus rather than against him results in a shaking, filling of the Spirit, and emboldened witness. "And when they had prayed, the place where they had gathered together was shaken, and they were all filled with the Holy Spirit and began to speak the word of God with boldness" (Acts 4:31).

In contrast to the powers and authorities who gather against God's servant, Jesus, his followers gather into a resisting community. Jesus first gathers them after his resurrection, commanding them not to leave Jerusalem, but to wait for what the Father had promised, "Which," he said, "you heard of from me; for John baptized with water, but you will be baptized with the Holy Spirit not many days from now" (Acts 1:4-5). Jesus then ascends to the Father, and the Spirit is poured out on the gathered believers at Pentecost, where they are empowered for mission. This gathering continues throughout Acts.[9]

The reported divine response following their intercession includes a physical shaking of the place, their being filled with the Holy Spirit, and their speaking of the word with boldness: "And when they had prayed, the place where they had gathered together was shaken, and they were all filled with the Holy Spirit and began to speak the word of God with boldness" (Acts 4:31).

The Greek term here used for shaking (*saleuō*)[10] is used throughout the Septuagint to describe judgment of the powers, including mountains (Judg. 5:5), and the whole earth.[11] One of the most pertinent texts regarding the judgment of the powers in the Old Testament is Psalm 82 (Psalm 81 in the Septuagint).

> God stands in the assembly of gods; and in the midst of them will judge gods. How long will ye judge unrighteously, and accept the persons of sinners? Judge the orphan and poor: do justice to the low and needy. Rescue the needy, and deliver the poor out of the hand of the sinner. They know not, nor understand; they walk on in darkness: all the foundations of the earth shall be shaken I have said, ye are gods; and all of you children of the Most High. But ye die as men, and fall as of the princes. Arise, O God, judge the earth: for thou shalt inherit all nations. (Ps. 81:1-8)[12]

Here the "foundations of the earth" are described as being shaken when God judges the "assembly of the gods" and "princes." Jesus himself speaks of a shaking of the powers of the heavens.

---

9. Acts 11:26; 13:44; 14:27: 15:6, 30; 20:7.

10. σαλεύω, *saleuō*, to waver, agitate, rock, topple, or (by implication) destroy; figuratively, to disturb, incite, move, shake (together), which can(not) be shaken.

11. Pss. 17:7; 59:2; 96:4; 98:1; 113:7.

12. Brenton, *Septuagint*.

> There will be signs in sun and moon and stars, and on the earth dismay among nations, in perplexity at the roaring of the sea and the waves, men fainting from fear and the expectation of the things which are coming upon the world; for the powers of the heavens will be shaken. (Luke 21:25-26)[13]

The shaking in response to the disciples' worship in the aftermath of persecution evokes another story in Acts that broadens the categories of powers that oppose the apostles and their proclamation of the Kingdom of God.

## PERSECUTION BY AND JUDGMENT OF THE POWERS IN ACTS 16

I often lead Bible studies about the story of Paul and Silas' missionary journey to Macedonia in Acts 16, both to examine how God leads people in ministry and how resistance to and opposition from the powers, and breakthrough, can happen.

In Acts 16, the apostles are moved by a special mix of divine guidance and their own initiative. As Paul and Silas advance on their missionary journey, Paul is "forbidden by the Holy Spirit to speak the word in Asia" (Acts 16:6). Next, the Spirit of Jesus does not permit them to go into Bithynia (Acts 16:7). As he and Silas continue to travel with no specific guidance, a vision appears to him in the night of a man from Macedonia standing and appealing to him to "come over to Macedonia and help us" (Acts 16:8). Paul and Silas set out immediately for Macedonia, "concluding that God had called us to preach the gospel to them" (Acts 16:10).

Paul and Silas appear to follow their own logic, heading straight for the leading city of Macedonia, Philippi (Acts 16:12). There, on the Sabbath, they go outside the gate of the city by the river "supposing that there would be a place of prayer" (Acts

---

13. See also Matt. 24:29; Mark 13:25; Heb. 12:26-27.

16:13). Outside the city gate,[14] several encounters take place that eventually lead to the Macedonian man.

First, they speak to a group of women who had come together, including Lydia of Thyatira, a seller of purple goods. The Lord opens her heart, and she and her household are baptized. She then welcomed them into her home (Acts 16:15-16).

The next day, Paul and Silas go further in their mission outside the gate. This time a slave girl,[15] who has "a spirit of a python," meets them (Acts 16:16). Like the lame man outside the Beautiful Gate, she takes the initiative in approaching the apostles. In contrast to the man who begs for money, she is described as "bringing her masters much profit by fortunetelling" (Acts 16:16). She is oppressed both as the slave by her masters who exploit her, and by an evil spirit that makes her profitable.

The slave girl is described as "having a spirit of divination" (literally a spirit of python). A python spirit was associated with a snake that guarded the Oracle of Delphi, which was viewed as the navel of the world. This spirit would have linked this girl directly with the most reputable source of spiritual and decision-making counsel in the ancient Greek world.[16]

For many days a slave girl followed Paul and Silas around, crying out: "these men are bond-servants [slaves] of the Most High God, who are proclaiming to you the way of salvation" (Acts 16:17). In calling them bond-servants (literally slaves) with no apparent fear, she may have been identifying with them in some way as a fellow slave. While it could look like this girl and the spirit empowering her was endorsing Paul and Silas, the girl says nothing of Jesus. The people would have viewed the Most High God as Zeus, and understood the girl as saying they were slaves of their (and her) god.

14. Here the term for gate (*pylē*) is used, which is also used with reference to the Beautiful Gate in Acts 3:10.

15. *Paidiskē* is the female diminutive of *paidos*, meaning "little slave girl."

16. Phthia was the High Priestess of the temple of Apollo, who was believed to empower the Oracle of Delphi.

Paul is greatly disturbed and casts the evil spirit out of her in the name of Jesus Christ (Acts 16:18). Exercising spiritual authority in Jesus' name shows the superior power of Jesus to python, and frees the little girl from what made her useful as a slave to her owners. Paul's invocation of the name of Jesus to expel a dominant regional spirit viewed as protecting the Oracle of Delphi reveals this stronghold's vulnerability. Binding the strong man allows his household to be pillaged, threatening the stakeholders and the system of rulers and authorities reigning in Philippi. As in Peter's confrontation with Jewish religious authorities in Acts 3, the apostles' exercising authority in Jesus' name to free the most vulnerable, weak, and oppressed person (in this case a demonized, enslaved little girl) unleashes serious persecution. The ensuing confrontation leads Paul and Silas straight to who I believe to be the Macedonian man of Paul's vision.

The first level of persecution comes from the slave-girl's masters (*kyrios*), who are outraged that they've lost their source of income.[17] "Their hope of profit[18] [the python spirit] was gone" (Acts 16:19). "They seized Paul and Silas and dragged them into the marketplace[19] before the authorities"[20] (Acts 16:19), the chief magistrates,[21] saying: "These men are throwing our city into confusion, being Jews, and are proclaiming customs which it is not lawful for us to accept or to observe, being Romans" (16:20-21).

The slave girl's masters charge Paul and Silas with throwing the whole city[22] into confusion. While at first glance this

17. The term for "income" or "profit" here is *ergasia*, which means "to make money or profit from one's business or activity" (Acts 19:24; Eph. 4:19). In this case, profits were directly related to a spirit of divination. Once deliverance occurred, the business activity was disempowered.

18. The term *elpis tē ergasia*, "hope for profit" is best interpreted as a religious, even idolatrous aspiration, *ergasia* (profit) being the power or "god."

19. *Agora.*

20. *Archōn.*

21. *Stratēgos* means "a civic commander, a governor (the name of the *duumviri* or highest magistrates in the municipia and colonies; they had the power of administering justice in the less important cases." Thayer, 4755.2.

22. The underlying Greek word here, *polis*, refers to a common New Testament macro power.

looks like a false accusation, there may be considerable truth to the charge. The casting out of a spirit that local people paid to consult, which they believed offered guidance for their decisions and destinies, truly threatened the spiritual underpinnings of the entire community and local economy. In talking through this story with two of Tierra Nueva's two Latino pastoral workers, my Latino colleagues identify *suerte* or luck related to gambling at local casinos or the lottery as dominant powers here. Meth and heroine dealers meet up with users who hang out at casinos that are open 24 hours a day. There they can get out of the cold and also gamble what they have in hopes of winning money that will buy more drugs.

The departure of the demonic spirit that empowered the masters' business brought confusion to the *polis* of Philippi. If a spiritual entity that lured people into gambling or contributed to a casino's profits could be cast out, Salvio and Julio insist that the exorcist would most certainly be persona non grata in the Skagit Valley. It is this kind of upset that Christians need to be ready to unleash as we announce and usher in the new community of Jesus' Kingdom today.

The owners of the slave girl attack Paul and Silas with the categories most readily available to them, those related to their visible racial/ethnic identity as Jews. "These men ... being Jews" (Acts 16:20). Anti-Semitism rears its head as Paul and Silas embody their highest calling as "sons of the prophets" who are here carrying out Abraham's covenant to bless every family of the earth, in alignment with Peter's earlier plea in the temple (Acts 3). They accuse them of proclaiming customs[23] "not lawful"[24] according to the dominant Roman system.

23. In the New Testament, the term "customs" (*ethos*) fits into the category of the non-human powers. They refer to Jewish religious practices (Luke 1:9; 2:42; 22:39; Acts 6:14; 15:1; 21:21: 26:3) and also Roman practices (Acts 16:21; 25:16).

24. This term, ἔξεστιν (lawful), is regularly used throughout the New Testament to refer to Jewish religious laws, which Jesus often transgresses (Matt. 12:2, 4, 10, 12; 14:4; 19:3; 20:15; 22:17; 27:6; Mark 2:24, 26; 3:4; 6:18; 10:2; 12:14; Luke 6:2, 4, 9; 14:3; 20:22; John 5:10; 18:31).

The crowd[25] then does something characteristically mob-like and rises up against them (Acts 16:22). The chief magistrates fully collaborate with the collective manifestation in response to the exorcism of the python in Jesus' name. They tear off Paul and Silas' robes, order them to be beaten with rods, "and when they had inflicted many blows upon them, they threw them into prison, commanding the jailer to guard them securely" (Acts 16:23).

Here we have the first reference in the story to an individual Macedonian man, who is commanded by the magistrates to guard them securely. The jailer subsequently "threw them into the inner prison, and fastened their feet in the stocks" (Acts 16:24). We are about to see how God's reign works to subvert, from the inside, the system that punishes God's representatives who offend it.

In reading this story with inmates, I sometimes ask them to identify the different antagonists mentioned in the story by their names, and what they do. People identify the masters, authorities, chief magistrates, and jailer, noting their actions of dragging them into the equivalent of the courts, racially profiling them as Jews, bringing them before the police, tearing off their clothes, ordering the punishment, beating them with rods, throwing them in jail (into the solitary confinement unit, commonly referred to as "the hole"), and fastening their feet in the stocks. We see that all of these antagonists are officials, and all their activities are negative towards the apostles.

Criminals are far more easily able to identify with this kind of harsh treatment and abuse by the authorities than most Christians. They sympathize with Paul and Silas and feel closer to them.

I ask the inmates what they think the lawmakers and the local courts are intending for law-breakers when they sentence criminals to jail or prison.

"They don't care about us. They just want to make money by filling their jails and prisons," someone says, expressing

---

25. The underlying Greek word *ochlos* is another category within the language of the powers in the Gospels and Acts.

a commonly held view. Other responses include: "control," "shame," "deprivation," and "punishment."

Let's see whether Paul and Silas let the punishments result in shaming and crushing them into submission. I ask someone to read Acts 16:25, "But about midnight Paul and Silas were praying and singing hymns of praise to God, and the prisoners were listening to them."

Paul and Silas appear to celebrate mistreatment at the hands of the authorities for having freed the slave girl. The men can understand that Paul and Silas would be praying, but do not understand why they would be singing hymns of praise to God. I invite them to read Matthew 5:10-12:

> Blessed are those who have been persecuted for the sake of righteousness, for theirs is the kingdom of heaven. Blessed are you when men cast insults at you, and persecute you, and say all kinds of evil against you falsely, on account of me. Rejoice, and be glad, for your reward in heaven is great, for so they persecuted the prophets who were before you.

The men are intrigued by the notion that following Jesus could be viewed as criminal behavior, and are able to identify with the fate of lawbreakers. Since they have already been maligned by the powers, they are more ready than most Christians for persecution for righteousness' sake. We also read Peter's words regarding unjust suffering in 1 Peter 4:12-16, as an invitation to a life that includes persecution for the sake of Jesus' name:

> Beloved, do not be surprised at the fiery ordeal among you, which comes upon you for your testing, as though some strange thing were happening to you; to the degree that you share the sufferings of Christ, keep on rejoicing, so that also at the revelation of his glory you may rejoice with exultation. If you are reviled for the name of Christ, you are blessed, because the Spirit of glory and of God rests on you. Make sure that none of you suffers as a murderer, or thief, or evildoer, or a troublesome meddler; but if anyone suffers as a

Christian, he is not to be ashamed, but is to glorify God in this name.[26]

I invite someone to read the next verse, which describes the impact of Paul and Silas' worship in prison.

And suddenly there came a great earthquake, so that the foundations of the prison house were shaken; and immediately all the doors were opened, and everyone's chains were unfastened (Acts 16:26)

There, in the jail, I ask inmates to summarize what happens in this verse and who benefits. The men describe the earthquake that shakes the foundations of the jail, popping the doors open and unfastening everyone's chains. I ask what the other prisoners were doing that would qualify them to benefit, and am surprised by someone's response: "They were listening to Paul and Silas pray and worship." It is encouraging to me that this simple communion between the apostles and their fellow prisoners who listen to them, is enough for everyone to benefit from the shaking that pops the doors and undoes the chains.

I point out what we've already seen in Acts 4, how when the first Christians praise God in response to the arrest and incarceration of Peter and John, the whole place where they were gathered was shaken. Worship of God in the face of persecution announces and unleashes God's judgment, shaking the foundations of the system.[27]

Next we look at the response of the man who occupies the place of law enforcer. He is the first and only individual man

26. See also 1 Pet. 2:19-20, "For this finds favor, if for the sake of conscience towards God a man bears up under sorrows when suffering unjustly. For what credit is there if, when you sin and are harshly treated, you endure it with patience? But if when you do what is right and suffer for it you patiently endure it, this finds favor with God."

27. Might Paul and Silas' liturgical resistance here embody a critical vocation of Jesus' followers, "to bring to light what is the administration of the mystery which for ages has been hidden in God, who created all things; in order that the manifold wisdom of God might now be made known through the church to the rulers and the authorities in the heavenly places" (Eph. 3:9-10).

from Macedonia who appears in the story, whom we have been looking for since a Macedonian man appeared to Paul in a vision that initiated his mission. An inmate reads Acts 16:27: "And when the jailer had been roused out of sleep and had seen the prison doors opened, he drew his sword and was about to kill himself, supposing that the prisoners had escaped."

We all note the behavior here which is foreign to us: a jailer about to take his life in response to what looks like a prison break. We talk about Paul, Silas, and the other prisoners' opportunity to be freed from their captor, benefiting from his potential suicide to make their escape. I wonder if the men will be disappointed as I invite someone to read Acts 16:28, "But Paul cried out with a loud voice, saying, 'Do yourself no harm, for we are all here!'"

Paul models remarkable authority in the midst of persecution, speaking words of life to the person embodying state power. In so doing, Paul reveals his (and our) unique agenda as a representative of Jesus' Kingdom. Crying out in a loud voice here evokes special spiritual authority, as when Jesus' raises Lazarus from the dead (John 11:43), and surrenders his spirit as he gives his life on the cross (Luke 23:46).[28] Paul shows no concern for his own freedom from his persecutor. Rather, he embodies care for the life of the jail official in a way that leads to a reversal of the normal power dynamic. Paul cares for the jailer who enforced the dominant system's harsh sentence. We continue reading Acts 4:29, which shows the impact of Paul's allegiance to Jesus on the jailer, "And he called for lights and rushed in and, trembling with fear, he fell down before Paul and Silas, and after he brought them out, he said, 'Sirs, what must I do to be saved?'"

---

28. Stephen cries out with a loud voice for God to not hold the sin of those who stone him against them (Acts 7:60). There are many other occurrences of crying out with a loud voice in the New Testament related to the worship of Jesus (Rev. 5:12; 7:10; 11:15; 12:10; 19:1). See Bob Ekblad, "Jesus' Subversive Victory Shouts in Matthew 27: Towards an empowering theology of the cross," in *The Bible in the Public Square: Reading the Signs of the Times*, ed. Cynthia Briggs Kittredge, Ellen Bradshaw Aitken, and Jonathan A. Draper (Minneapolis: Fortress, 2008), 143-156.

Rather than rushing in to apprehend his prisoners, the terrified jailer surrenders to Paul and Silas, falling down before them in fear and trembling. The jailer brings them out of confinement. In response to their intervention to save his life, he asks them what he himself must do to be saved. Paul and Silas present Jesus to the Macedonian man, regardless of his official role as law enforcer. They call the jailer to believe in the Lord Jesus, suggesting that he replace the dominant lord, Caesar, with Jesus as his highest power. They share the message to him and his household, saying, "'Believe in the Lord Jesus, and you shall be saved, you and your household.' And they spoke the word of the Lord to him together with all who were in his house" (Acts 16:31-32).

The jailer responds by caring for their physical needs and immediately heeding their call to conversion and baptism. "And he took them that very hour of the night and washed their wounds, and immediately he was baptized, he and all his household. And he brought them into his house and set food before them, and rejoiced greatly, having believed in God with his whole household" (Acts 16:33-34).

While the story shows a positive outcome for Jesus' followers incarcerated unjustly, it falls short of offering hope to ordinary criminals for immediate release, as there is no visible benefit to Paul and Silas' fellow prisoners. The other prisoners do not yet appear to be included in the jailer's hospitality. It is only the apostles themselves, who appear to be unjustly punished, who experience visible benefits. Yet, on every occasion I have read this story with inmates, the men express a longing to move in the opposite spirit of the misery their punishment is meant to inflict, and to confess any sin that landed them in jail.

"We all need to start studying the Bible every night together in our pod," says Jeff to his fellow gang members. We talk about the value of prayer, giving thanks to God, and worship in the midst of pain and suffering. When time allows, we continue reading together. The ending of this story brings hope to prisoners who have often themselves suffered injustices in the courts.

Even before their release, the apostles confront abusive authorities, holding them accountable for their injustices.

## CHALLENGING THE POWERS

When the chief magistrates send policemen to tell the jailer to release Paul and Silas, Paul boldly confronts their abuse of power, "They have beaten us in public without trial, men who are Romans, and have thrown us into prison; and now are they sending us away secretly? No indeed! But let them come themselves and bring us out" (Acts 16:37).

Paul requires the higher officials, the chief magistrates, to come and bring them out of prison themselves rather then sending the lower-level policemen. Paul's appeal to his rights as a Roman citizen models an appropriate civic posture. The apostles call the human officials who represent the local *polis* to be accountable to the overarching laws of the Roman Empire. In this case, they advocate for themselves using the legal system, requiring officials to behave in ways that make the macro powers serve them as they were created to serve.[29] Paul's appeal to his legal rights as a Roman strike fear into the hearts of the officials, who bring them out of jail and beg them to leave their city (Acts 16:38-39). Paul and Silas know their rights and refuse to comply immediately. They demonstrate freedom to resist the officials in their decision to visit the new believers of Philippi before leaving: "They went out of the prison and entered the house of Lydia, and when they saw the brethren, they encouraged them and departed" (Acts 16:40).

Paul and Silas are more concerned about reconnecting with and encouraging the new believers than immediately complying with the authorities. Only after completing their original

29. Gen. 1:26-28 presents humans as made in God's image and likeness, given authority to subdue the earth and rule over the non-human creation. Ps. 8 and its appropriation by New Testament writers show the non-human creation as being placed under humanity's feet, which is accomplished through Jesus death, resurrection, and ascension.

mission to Macedonia do they depart for their next assignment in Thessalonica and beyond. Like Peter and John, we see a single-minded focus on their engagements in the Kingdom of God.

## THE CHURCH AS RESISTING COMMUNITY

Peter and John, and Paul and Silas model Christian engagement with religious and secular powers in the midst of the larger mission to announce and embody Jesus' Kingdom. Peter and John and their companions worship and make prophetic declarations in the face of persecution from Jewish religious rulers and authorities in Acts 4. Healing, signs, and wonders confirm the apostles' allegiance to Jesus, celebrated as they gather in the alternative community of strangers and aliens. The shaking of the gathering places and infilling of the Spirit brings freedom from fear of threats of imprisonment, and later from literal jail doors and shackles, for the benefit of a pagan jailer and his family. In both cases, new boldness rises for the illegal proclamation of Jesus.

Our story of the healing of the man lame from birth in Acts 3-4 ends in a depiction of the early church community reminiscent of the gathering of believers out of which Peter and John set out towards the Beautiful Gate in Acts 2:43-47. This community has the markings of vibrancy and otherness that inspires me to want to live in this newness now.

The grouping of those who believe in Jesus is called a *plēthos*, meaning fullness, large number, or multitude. This contrasts with the myriad of titles distinguishing different rulers and authorities according to their institutional identities. The writer of Acts offers a picture of unity and solidarity "not of this world," in contrast to the distinctions of titles, social class, and financial status that characterizes the world under the domination of rulers and authorities.

> The congregation of those who believed were of one heart and soul; and not one of them claimed that anything belonging to him was his own, but all things were common property to them. (Acts 4:32-33)

The power of God was manifested to confirm the apostles' witness regarding Jesus, a power different from that of the Jewish religious system or the State.

> And with great power the apostles were giving testimony to the resurrection of the Lord Jesus, and abundant grace was upon them all. For there was not a needy person among them, for all who were owners of land or houses would sell them and bring the proceeds of the sales and lay them at the apostles' feet, and they would be distributed to each as any had need. (Acts 4:34-35)

Resurrection power was manifested through the apostles as they proclaimed Jesus' resurrection from the dead. They announced that Jesus, whom the religious and state powers had killed by death penalty, was alive and active. Furthermore, this Jesus was being proclaimed and embodied through his multiplying followers. This alternative community grew constantly in the face of threats and imprisonment. People were attracted to the Jesus movement, as "all the more believers in the Lord, multitudes of men and women, were constantly added to their number" (Acts 5:14). This new community experienced the very works of Jesus in full continuity with Jesus' own earthly ministry in the Gospels. May this inspire us to raise the bar for normal practice now, as we live within this same period before Jesus' second coming.

> To such an extent that they even carried the sick out into the streets and laid them on cots and pallets, so that when Peter came by at least his shadow might fall on any one of them. Also the people from the cities in the vicinity of Jerusalem were coming together, bringing people who were sick or afflicted with unclean spirits, and they were all being healed. (Acts 5:15-16)

Building Christian community as a secure, permanent institution is not what we see happening in Acts, nor should it be our focus now. Christian community prepares for and propels mission. It is out of the gathered community that Peter, John,

Stephen, Philip, Paul, Silas, you, and I depart for the *beautiful gate* sites where Jesus' Kingdom advances, finding, saving, and bringing home the lost sheep.

There, between the gathered community and the religious institutions or sacred places, outside the gate, we make ourselves available for transformational encounters. We act in the name of Jesus, who died outside the gate for the sins of the world (Heb. 13:12). We move in the authority of our attachment to Jesus, and represent him and his Kingdom, and no other name. "There is salvation in no one else; for there is no other name under heaven that has been given among men by which we must be saved" (Acts 4:12).

In the power of his resurrection life, we heal the sick, cast out demons, and raise the dead. Like Jesus, who saves us while we were yet sinners, we cross people over the lines and borders and through the gates that exclude into the newness of life where they reclaim their identity, inheritance, and vocation as the Father's beloved. We accompany people, not to make them fully endowed citizens of this world, but to bear witness to a kingdom not of this world, here, but still to come. In the heart of places of power and privilege, we bear witness to the only one who saves, Jesus Christ.

We bear witness to Jesus as the saving, victorious victim from amongst those who exclude and kill. We expose the mechanisms of rebellion, exclusion, and death, and call people to confession, repentance, and conversion. We declare people's sins forgiven, and invite the Spirit's presence that cleanses, refreshes, and empowers.

We invite people outside the comfortable confines of the temples of our time into the high calling of Abraham's seed: to be a blessing to all families of the world. And in the midst of this activity, and in continuity with the experience of the first apostles, we mustn't be surprised if persecution follows.

Resistance from the powers and those who defend them can be expected and must be prepared for. Throughout the world, Christians are experiencing persecution, including incarceration and martyrdom. The gathered community is scattered over and over again, [30] as the sower casts his seed onto the heavily-worn paths, the rocky and weed-filled soils, in search of good soil where it will take root and bear fruit. This scattering propels Jesus' disciples out of Jerusalem and Judea into Samaria and the ends of the earth.

Jesus' followers who gather to worship the resurrected King are empowered for mission. Will you make yourself available? Will you surrender to Jesus and this beautiful call? Whether you are sent out, cast out, or scattered through persecution, the Kingdom of God advances. May you venture out in confidence towards new *beautiful gates* across any and every line the Spirit calls you to cross. May you step out with open eyes, ready to spot and enter into divinely orchestrated relationships that will bring heaven to earth. May you proclaim the good news with boldness in the face of resistance, and experience the joy of witnessing Jesus' resurrected presence with you, confirming your words with the signs that follow.

---

30. Continue reading Acts 5:17–8:3.

# Bibliography

Allen, John. "Destroy the Islamic State Now." Last modified August 20, 2014. http://www.defenseone.com/ideas/2014/08/gen-allen-destroy-islamic-state-now/92012/.

Anonymous. *The Way of a Pilgrim and The Pilgrim Continues His Way*. Translated by Olga Savin. Boston: Shambhala Publications, 2001.

———. "What is cross theology / theology of the cross?" http://www.gotquestions.org/cross-theology.html

Bauer, William. *A Greek-English Lexicon of the New Testament and other Early Christian Literature*. Translated by William F. Arndt and F. Wilbur Gingrich. Chicago: University of Chicago, 1979.

Brenton, Lancelot C. L., trans. *Septuagint*. London: Samuel Bagster & Sons, 1851.

Thayer, Joseph Henrey, and Buttmann, Alexander. *A Grammar of the New Testament Greek*. Primary Source Edition. Charleston: Nabu Press, 2013.

Ekblad, Bob. "Jesus' Subersive Victory Shouts in Matthew 27: Towards an empowering theology of the cross." In *The Bible in the Public Square: Reading the Signs of the Times*, edited by Cynthia Briggs Kittredge, Ellen Bradshaw Aitken, and Jonathan A. Draper, 143-156. Minneapolis: Fortress, 2008.

———. *A New Christian Manifesto: Pledging Allegiance to the Kingdom of God*. Louisville: Westminster John Knox, 2008.

Ekblad, Eugene Robert, Jr. *Isaiah's Servant Poems According to the Septuagint: An Exegetical and Theological Study*. Leuven: Peeters, 1999.

Forde, Gerhard. "On Being a Theologian of the Cross." http://www.religion-online.org/showarticle.asp?title=320.

Hall, John Douglass. *The Cross in Our Context: Jesus and the Suffering World*. Minneapolis: Fortress, 2003.

Hausherr, Irénée. *The Name of Jesus*. Translated by Charles Cummings. Michigan: Cistercian Publications, 1978.

St. Hesychios the Priest, "On Watchfulness and Holiness." In *The Philokalia: The Complete Text*, vol. 1, 161-198. Translated by G. E. H. Palmer, Philip Sherrard, and Kallistos Ware. London: Faber and Faber, 1979.

Kadloubovsky, E. and G.E.H. Palmer, trans. *The Writings from the Philokalia on the Prayer of the Heart*. London: Faber and Faber, 1992.

Louw, J. P. and Eugene Albert Nida, eds. *Greek-English Lexicon of the New Testament*. New York: United Bible Society, 1988. Accordance Bible Software.

A Monk of the Eastern Church [Fr. Lev Gillet]. *The Jesus Prayer*. Crestwood: St. Vladimir's Seminary Press, 1987.

Thayer, Joseph Henry. *Thayer's Greek-English Lexicon of the New Testament*. New York: Harper & Brothers, 1889. Accordance Bible Software.

Trueman, Carl R. "Luther's Theology of the Cross." http://www.opc.org/new_horizons/NH05/10b.html.